PRACTICE - ASSESS - DIAGNOSE

I0890432

180 Days of WRITING for Third Grade

Author
Kristi Sturgeon

Shell Education

Standards

For information on how this resource meets national and other state standards, see pages 4–6. You may also review this information by scanning the QR code or visiting our website at http://www.shelleducation.com and following the on-screen directions.

Publishing Credits

Corinne Burton, M.A.Ed., *President*; Emily R. Smith, M.A.Ed., *Content Director*; Jennifer Wilson, *Editor*; Grace Alba Le, *Multimedia Designer*; Don Tran, *Production Artist*; Stephanie Bernard, *Assistant Editor*; Amber Goff, *Editorial Assistant*

Image Credits

pp. 47, 61, 64, 66, 69, 85–88, 95, 101–102, 111, 113–115, 156, 172, 191–192, 213–214: iStock; All other images Shutterstock

Standards

© Copyright 2010. National Governors Association Center for Best Practices and Council of Chief State School Officers. All rights reserved. (CCSS)

Shell Education
5482 Argosy Avenue
Huntington Beach, CA 92649-1030
www.tcmpub.com/shell-education
ISBN 978-1-4258-1526-4
© 2015 Shell Education Publishing, Inc.
Printed by: 51497
Printed in: China

The classroom teacher may reproduce copies of materials in this book for classroom use only. The reproduction of any part for an entire school or school system is strictly prohibited. No part of this publication may be transmitted, stored, or recorded in any form without written permission from the publisher.

TABLE OF CONTENTS

INTRODUCTION

The Need for Practice

To be successful in today's writing classrooms, students must deeply understand both concepts and procedures so that they can discuss and demonstrate their understanding. Demonstrating understanding is a process that must be continually practiced for students to be successful. Practice is especially important to help students apply their concrete, conceptual understanding of each particular writing skill.

Understanding Assessment

In addition to providing opportunities for frequent practice, teachers must be able to assess students' writing skills. This is important so that teachers can adequately address students' misconceptions, build on their current understandings, and challenge them appropriately. Assessment is a long-term process that involves careful analysis of student responses from a discussion, project, practice sheet, or test. When analyzing the data, it is important for teachers to reflect on how their teaching practices may have influenced students' responses and to identify those areas where additional instruction may be required. In short, the data gathered from assessments should be used to inform instruction: slow down, speed up, or reteach. This type of assessment is called *formative assessment.*

HOW TO USE THIS BOOK

With *180 Days of Writing*, creative, theme-based units guide students as they practice the five steps of the writing process: prewriting, drafting, revising, editing, and publishing. During each odd week (Weeks 1, 3, 5, etc.), students interact with mentor texts. Then, students apply their learning by writing their own pieces during each following even week (Weeks 2, 4, 6, etc.). Many practice pages also focus on grammar/language standards to help improve students' writing.

Easy to Use and Standards Based

These daily activities reinforce grade-level skills across the various genres of writing: opinion, informative/explanatory, and narrative. Each day provides a full practice page, making the activities easy to prepare and implement as part of a classroom morning routine, at the beginning of each writing lesson, or as homework.

The chart below indicates the writing and language standards that are addressed throughout this book. See pages 5–6 for a breakdown of which writing standard is covered in each week. **Note:** Students may not have deep understandings of some topics in this book. Remember to assess students based on their writing skills and not their content knowledge.

College and Career Readiness Standards

Writing 3.1—Write opinion pieces on topics or texts, supporting a point of view with reasons.
Writing 3.2—Write informative/explanatory texts to examine a topic and convey ideas and information clearly.
Writing 3.3—Write narratives to develop real or imagined experiences or events using elective technique, descriptive details, and clear event sequences
Language 3.1—Demonstrate command of the conventions of standard English grammar and usage when writing or speaking.
Language 3.2—Demonstrate command of the conventions of standard English capitalization, punctuation, and spelling when writing.
Language 3.4—Determine or clarify the meaning of unknown and multiple-meaning words and phrases based on *grade 3 reading and content,* choosing flexibly from a range of strategies
Language 3.5—Demonstrate understanding of word relationships and nuances in word meanings.

 © Shell Education

HOW TO USE THIS BOOK *(cont.)*

Below is a list of overarching themes, corresponding weekly themes, and the writing standards that students will encounter throughout this book. For each overarching theme, students will interact with mentor texts in the odd week and then apply their learning by writing their own pieces in the even week. **Note:** The writing prompts for each week can be found on pages 7–8. You may wish to display the prompts in the classroom for students to reference throughout the appropriate weeks.

Overarching Themes	Weekly Themes	Standards
Biomes	**Week 1:** Desert Animals **Week 2:** Tundra Animals	**Writing 3.2**—Write informative/explanatory texts to examine a topic and convey ideas and information clearly.
Seasons	**Week 3:** Summer/Fall **Week 4:** Winter/Spring	**Writing 3.1**—Write opinion pieces on topics or texts, supporting a point of view with reasons.
Animals	**Week 5:** Wild Animals **Week 6:** Pets	**Writing 3.1**—Write opinion pieces on topics or texts, supporting a point of view with reasons.
Geography	**Week 7:** Continents **Week 8:** Bodies of Water	**Writing 3.2**—Write informative/explanatory texts to examine a topic and convey ideas and information clearly.
Traditions	**Week 9:** Birthdays **Week 10:** Holidays	**Writing 3.3**—Write narratives to develop real or imagined experiences or events using elective technique, descriptive details, and clear event sequences.
Natural Disasters	**Week 11:** Tornadoes **Week 12:** Earthquakes	**Writing 3.2**—Write informative/explanatory texts to examine a topic and convey ideas and information clearly.
Travel	**Week 13:** Air Travel **Week 14:** Land Travel	**Writing 3.3**—Write narratives to develop real or imagined experiences or events using elective technique, descriptive details, and clear event sequences.
Superheroes	**Week 15:** Superheroes **Week 16:** Villains	**Writing 3.1**—Write opinion pieces on topics or texts, supporting a point of view with reasons.
Wonders of the World	**Week 17:** Grand Canyon **Week 18:** Egyptian Pyramids	**Writing 3.2**—Write informative/explanatory texts to examine a topic and convey ideas and information clearly.

HOW TO USE THIS BOOK *(cont.)*

Overarching Themes	Weekly Themes	Standards
Inventors	**Week 19:** Thomas Edison **Week 20:** Benjamin Franklin	**Writing 3.3**—Write narratives to develop real or imagined experiences or events using elective technique, descriptive details, and clear event sequences.
Under the Sea	**Week 21:** Octopuses **Week 22:** Sharks	**Writing 3.2**—Write informative/explanatory texts to examine a topic and convey ideas and information clearly.
Solar System	**Week 23:** Planets **Week 24:** Sun and Moon	**Writing 3.2**—Write informative/explanatory texts to examine a topic and convey ideas and information clearly.
Famous Authors	**Week 25:** Eric Carle **Week 26:** J.K. Rowling	**Writing 3.3**—Write narratives to develop real or imagined experiences or events using elective technique, descriptive details, and clear event sequences.
Insects	**Week 27:** Butterflies **Week 28:** Bees	**Writing 3.1**—Write opinion pieces on topics or texts, supporting a point of view with reasons.
Desserts	**Week 29:** Cookies **Week 30:** Ice Cream	**Writing 3.1**—Write opinion pieces on topics or texts, supporting a point of view with reasons.
Volcanoes	**Week 31:** Active Volcanoes **Week 32:** Dormant Volcanoes	**Writing 3.3**—Write narratives to develop real or imagined experiences or events using elective technique, descriptive details, and clear event sequences.
The Great Outdoors	**Week 33:** Hiking **Week 34:** Camping	**Writing 3.1**—Write opinion pieces on topics or texts, supporting a point of view with reasons.
Government Offices	**Week 35:** Public Library **Week 36:** Post Office	**Writing 3.3**—Write narratives to develop real or imagined experiences or events using elective technique, descriptive details, and clear event sequences.

© Shell Education

HOW TO USE THIS BOOK *(cont.)*

Weekly Setup

Write each prompt on the board throughout the appropriate week. Students should reference the prompts as they work through the activity pages so that they stay focused on the topics and the right genre of writing: opinion, informative/explanatory, and narrative. You may wish to print copies of this chart from the digital resources (filename: G3_writingprompts.pdf) and distribute them to students to keep throughout the school year.

Week	Prompt
1	Describe the types of animals that live in a desert. Include specific facts about how the animals adapt and live in the environment.
2	Describe the types of animals that live in a tundra. Include specific facts about how the animals adapt and live in the environment.
3	It's a contest! Fall and summer both think they're the better season. Which season will you support? Provide reasons to support your opinion.
4	It's a contest! Winter and spring both think they're the better season. Which season will you support? Provide reasons to support your opinion.
5	Write an opinion paragraph about which wild animal you like best. Be sure to include descriptive adjectives to help support your opinion.
6	Write an opinion paragraph about which animal you think makes the best pet. Be sure to include descriptive adjectives to help support your opinion.
7	Write an informative/explanatory paragraph about continents. Include at least two continents in your writing and explain unique features of each one.
8	Write an informative/explanatory paragraph about bodies of water. Include at least two types of bodies of water, and explain what each one looks like.

Week	Prompt
9	Imagine that you are having a birthday party. Write a narrative paragraph to describe the celebration. Include details about how you prepare for the party and what happens at the party.
10	Think about a holiday you have celebrated. Describe the celebration. Include at least two lines of dialogue.
11	Think about tornadoes. Write an informative/explanatory paragraph about tornadoes. Include facts about how they begin and what destruction they can cause.
12	Think about earthquakes. Write an informative/explanatory paragraph about earthquakes. Include facts about how they begin and what destruction they can cause.
13	Imagine traveling somewhere by air. Describe your experience. Be sure to include characters, setting, problem(s), rising action, and a solution.
14	Imagine traveling somewhere by land. Describe your experience. Be sure to include characters, setting, problem(s), rising action, and a solution.
15	Do you like superheroes? Write an opinion paragraph about whether or not superheroes are a good thing. Include at least three reasons to support your opinion.
16	Everyone seems to always root for superheroes. People think villains are too evil to support. Write an opinion paragraph stating why we should understand villains' perspectives.

HOW TO USE THIS BOOK *(cont.)*

Week	Prompt
17	Think about the Grand Canyon. Write an informative/explanatory paragraph about the Grand Canyon. Include facts about what you can find there.
18	Think about Egyptian pyramids. Write an informative/explanatory paragraph about Egyptian pyramids. Include facts about what they look like and how they are used.
19	Write a narrative paragraph about meeting Thomas Edison. Include details about his invention of the lightbulb.
20	Write a narrative paragraph about meeting Benjamin Franklin. Include details about what happened when you met him.
21	Think about octopuses. Write an informative/explanatory paragraph about octopuses. Include facts about how they protect themselves from predators.
22	Think about sharks. Write an informative/explanatory paragraph about sharks. Include facts about what they eat and what they look like.
23	Think about the planets. Write an informative/explanatory paragraph about the planets. Include details about some of the planets in our solar system.
24	Think about the sun and the moon. Write an informative/explanatory paragraph about the most interesting facts about them. Discuss their similarities and differences, too.
25	Imagine you are interviewing Eric Carle. What would you ask him? What would you discuss? Write a made-up dialogue between the two of you. Include at least three questions with corresponding answers.
26	Imagine you are interviewing J.K. Rowling. What would you ask her? What would you discuss? Write a made-up dialogue between the two of you. Include at least three questions with corresponding answers.

Week	Prompt
27	Do you think butterflies are amazing insects? Explain why you do or do not think they are amazing. Give at least three reasons to support your opinion.
28	Do you think bees are interesting? Write a paragraph expressing your opinion. Give at least three reasons to support your opinion.
29	Do you like cookies? Explain why you do or do not like them. Give at least three reasons to support your opinion.
30	Do you think ice cream is the best dessert? Write an opinion paragraph about explaining your thoughts. Give at least three reasons to support your opinion.
31	Imagine that your teacher is going to teach you about active volcanoes. Write a narrative paragraph about your experience. Remember to write in sequential order.
32	Imagine you are near a dormant volcano. Write a narrative paragraph about your experience. Remember to write in sequential order.
33	Do you like hiking? Write an opinion paragraph explaining why you do or do not enjoy hiking. Include at least three reasons to support your opinion.
34	Do you like camping? Write an opinion paragraph explaining why you do or do not like camping. Include at least three reasons to support your opinion.
35	Imagine that you are going on a trip to the public library. Write a narrative paragraph to describe how the trip goes. Include details about the events that happen while on the trip.
36	Imagine that you need to mail a package and have just arrived at the post office. What do you do next? How do you make sure your package gets mailed? Write a narrative about your experience.

HOW TO USE THIS BOOK *(cont.)*

Using the Practice Pages

The activity pages provide practice and assessment opportunities for each day of the school year. Teachers may wish to prepare packets of weekly practice pages for the classroom or for homework. As outlined on pages 5–6, each two-week unit is aligned to one writing standard. **Note:** Before implementing each week's activity pages, review the corresponding prompt on pages 7–8 with students and have students brainstorm thoughts about each topic.

On odd weeks, students practice the daily skills using mentor texts. On even weeks, students use what they have learned in the previous week and apply it to their own writing.

Each day focuses on one of the steps in the writing process: prewriting, drafting, revising, editing, and publishing.

There are 18 overarching themes. Each odd week and the following even week focus on unique themes that fit under one overarching theme. For a list of the overarching themes and individual weekly themes, see pages 5–6.

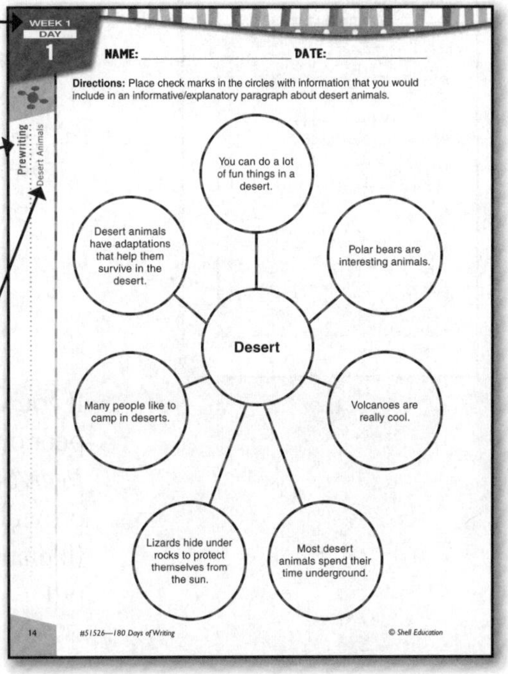

Using the Resources

The following resources will be helpful to students as they complete the activity pages. Print copies of these resources and provide them to students to keep at their desks.

Rubrics for the three genres of writing (opinion, informative/explanatory, and narrative) can be found on pages 202–204. Use the rubrics to assess students' writing at the end of each even week. Be sure to share these rubrics with students often so that they know what is expected of them.

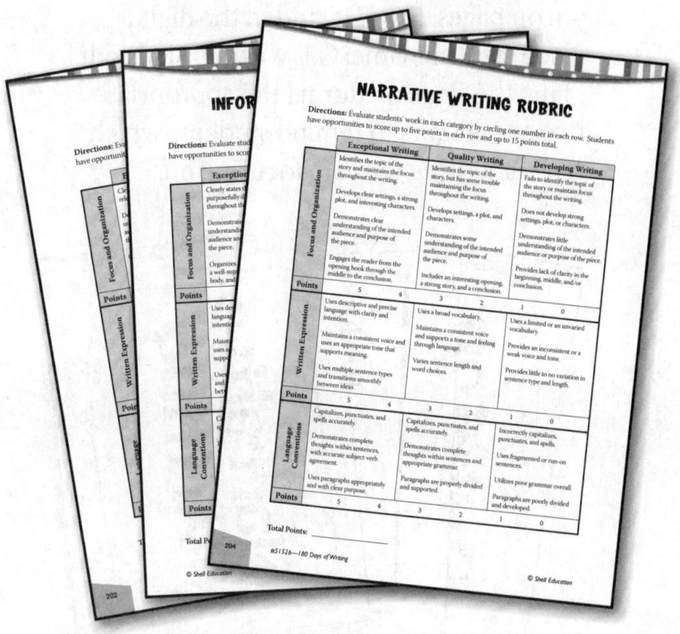

HOW TO USE THIS BOOK *(cont.)*

Using the Resources *(cont.)*

The Writing Process can be found on page 208 and in the digital resources (filename: G3_writing_process.pdf). Students can reference each step of the writing process as they move through each week.

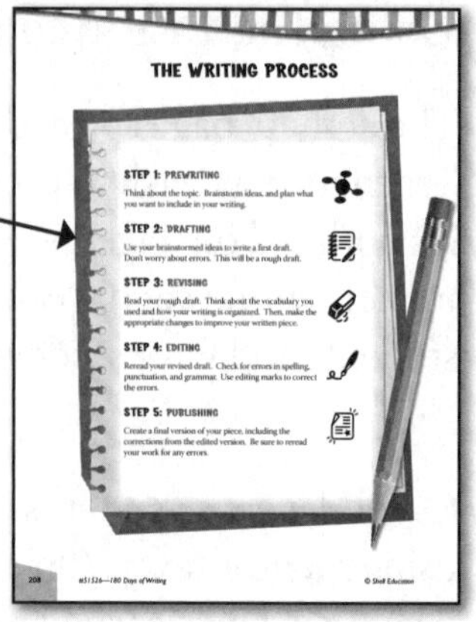

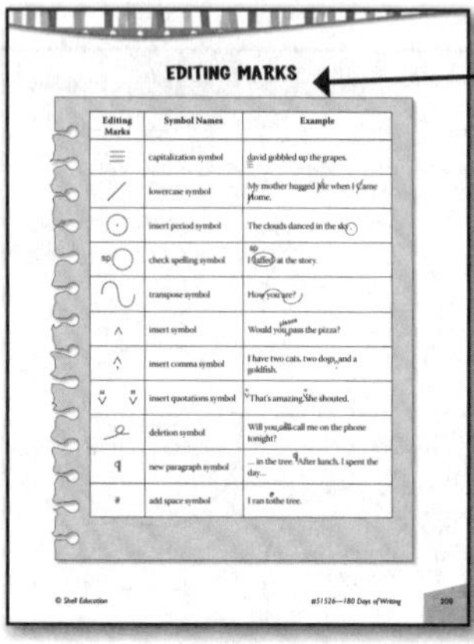

Editing Marks can be found on page 209 and in the digital resources (filename: G3_editing_marks.pdf). Students may need to reference this page as they work on the editing activities (Day 4s).

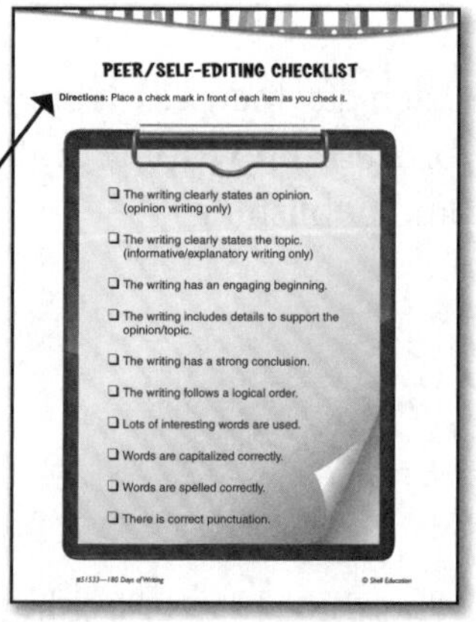

If you wish to have students peer or self-edit their writing, a *Peer/Self-Editing Checklist* is provided in the digital resources (filename: G3_peer_checklist.pdf).

Writing Signs for each of the writing genres are on pages 213–215 and in the digital resources (filename: G3_writing_signs.pdf). Hang the signs up during the appropriate two-week units to remind students which type of writing they are focusing on.

Writing Tips pages for each of the writing genres can be found on pages 210–212 and in the digital resources (filename: G3_writing_tips.pdf). Students can reference the appropriate *Writing Tips* pages as they work through the weeks.

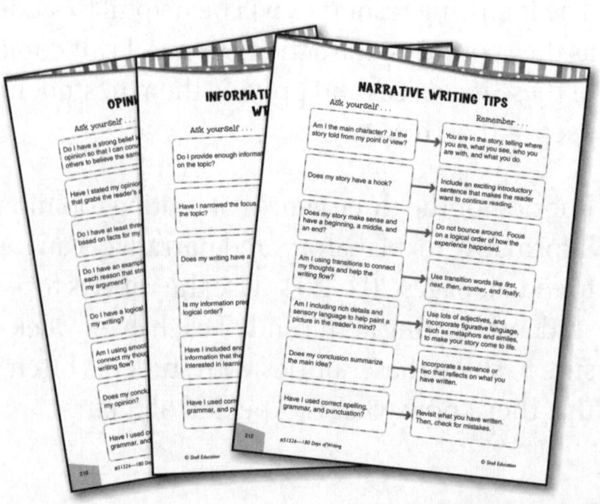

HOW TO USE THIS BOOK *(cont.)*

Diagnostic Assessment

Teachers can use the practice pages as diagnostic assessments. The data analysis tools included with the book enable teachers or parents to quickly score students' work and monitor their progress. Teachers and parents can quickly see which writing skills students may need to target further to develop proficiency.

After students complete each two-week unit, score each students' even week Day 5 published piece using the appropriate, genre-specific rubric (pages 202–204). Then, complete the *Practice Page Item Analysis* (pages 205–207) that matches the writing genre. These charts are also provided in the digital resources (filenames: G3_opinion_analysis.pdf, G3_inform_analysis.pdf, G3_narrative_analysis.pdf). Teachers can input data into the electronic files directly on the computer, or they can print the pages and analyze students' work using paper and pencil.

To Complete the Practice Page Item Analyses:

- Write or type students' names in the far-left column. Depending on the number of students, more than one copy of the form may be needed, or you may need to add rows.
- The weeks in which the particular writing genres are the focus are indicated across the tops of the charts. **Note:** Students are only assessed on the even weeks, therefore the odd weeks are not included on the charts.
- For each student, record his or her rubric score in the appropriate column.
- Add the scores for each student after they've focused on a particular writing genre twice. Place that sum in the far right column. Use these scores as benchmarks to determine how each student is performing. This allows for three benchmarks during the year that you can use to gather formative diagnostic data.

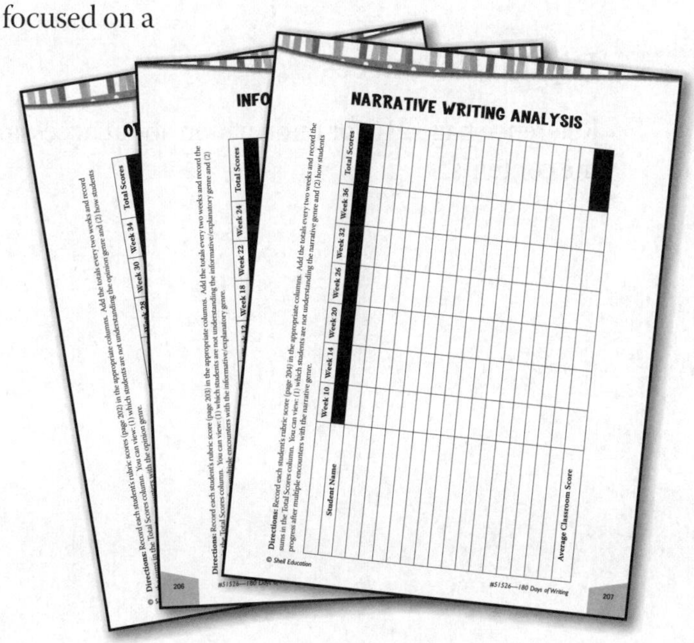

HOW TO USE THIS BOOK *(cont.)*

Using the Results to Differentiate Instruction

Once results are gathered and analyzed, teachers can use the results to inform the way they differentiate instruction. The data can help determine which writing types are the most difficult for students and which students need additional instructional support and continued practice.

Whole-Class Support

The results of the diagnostic analysis may show that the entire class is struggling with a particular writing genre. If these concepts have been taught in the past, this indicates that further instruction or reteaching is necessary. If these concepts have not been taught in the past, this data is a great preassessment and may demonstrate that students do not have a working knowledge of the concepts. Thus, careful planning for the length of the unit(s) or lesson(s) must be considered, and additional front-loading may be required.

Small-Group or Individual Support

The results of the diagnostic analysis may show that an individual student or a small group of students is struggling with a particular writing genre. If these concepts have been taught in the past, this indicates that further instruction or reteaching is necessary. Consider pulling these students aside to instruct them further on the concept(s) while others are working independently. Students may also benefit from extra practice using games or computer-based resources. Teachers can also use the results to help identify individual students or groups of proficient students who are ready for enrichment or above-grade-level instruction. These students may benefit from independent learning contracts or more challenging activities.

Digital Resources

Reference page 216 for information about accessing the digital resources and an overview of the contents.

© Shell Education

STANDARDS CORRELATIONS

Shell Education is committed to producing educational materials that are research and standards based. In this effort, we have correlated all of our products to the academic standards of all 50 states, the District of Columbia, the Department of Defense Dependents Schools, and all Canadian provinces.

How to Find Standards Correlations

To print a customized correlation report of this product for your state, visit our website at **www.tcmpub.com/shell-education** and follow the on-screen directions. If you require assistance in printing correlation reports, please contact our Customer Service Department at 1-877-777-3450.

Purpose and Intent of Standards

Legislation mandates that all states adopt academic standards that identify the skills students will learn in kindergarten through grade twelve. Many states also have standards for Pre-K. This same legislation sets requirements to ensure the standards are detailed and comprehensive.

Standards are designed to focus instruction and guide adoption of curricula. Standards are statements that describe the criteria necessary for students to meet specific academic goals. They define the knowledge, skills, and content students should acquire at each level. Standards are also used to develop standardized tests to evaluate students' academic progress.

Teachers are required to demonstrate how their lessons meet state standards. State standards are used in the development of all of our products, so educators can be assured they meet the academic requirements of each state.

The activities in this book are aligned to today's national and state-specific college and career readiness standards. The chart on page 4 lists the writing and language standards used throughout this book. A more detailed chart on pages 5–6 correlates the specific writing standards to each week.

NAME: ______________________ **DATE:** ________________

Directions: Place check marks in the circles with information that you would include in an informative/explanatory paragraph about desert animals.

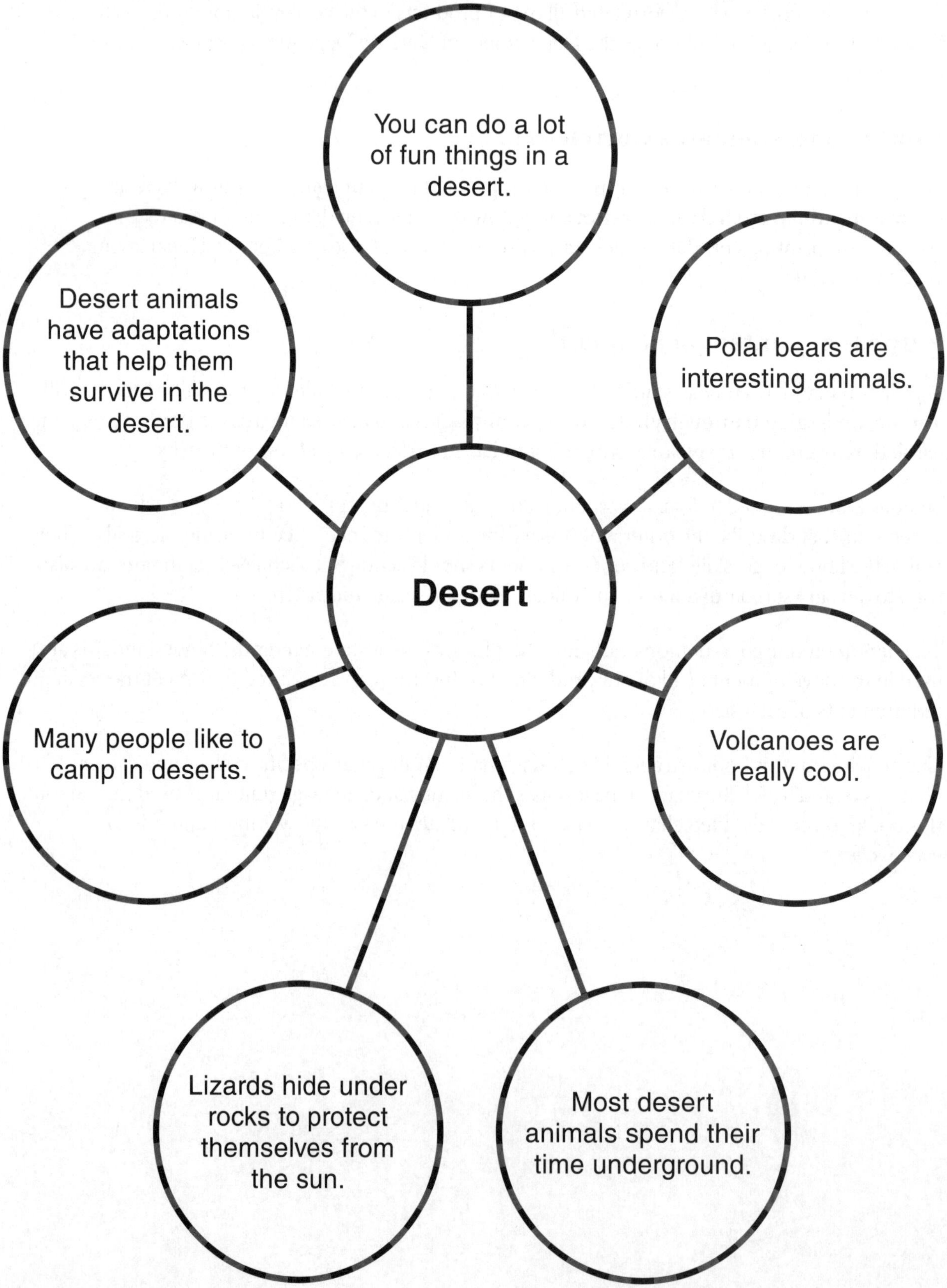

 © Shell Education

NAME: ______________________ **DATE:** ______________

Drafting
Desert Animals

Directions: Read the informative/explanatory paragraph about desert animals. Then, answer the questions.

Desert animals must adapt to extreme heat and lack of water. Several animals are active only at night because of the daytime heat. Some animals don't need to drink any water. They get enough from the plants and seeds they eat. Several desert animals do not have sweat glands, allowing them to hold in more moisture throughout the day. Birds have feathers to help keep them cool and covered during the day.

1. What is the topic sentence?

____

____

2. How can the author improve the paragraph?

____

____

____

____

____

____

Remember!

A strong informative/explanatory paragraph should include:

- a topic sentence
- three details to support the main idea
- a concluding sentence

Printing Practice abc

Directions: Use your best printing to write two adjectives about desert animals.

____

____

NAME: ______________________ **DATE:** ______________

Directions: Read the sentences. The subjects are correct, but some of the verbs are not. Write *C* if a sentence is correct. Write *I* if a sentence is incorrect. Correct any incorrect verbs on the lines.

_____ **1.** Scientists study desert animals.

____

_____ **2.** The camels travels over the sand dune.

____

_____ **3.** The lizard bury himself under a rock.

____

_____ **4.** A desert animal adapt to its surroundings.

____

Boost Your Learning!

Subject-verb agreement means that the subject and verb need to match each other in number. If a subject is singular, the verb should be singular. If a subject is plural, the verb should be plural.

Examples

- The **hiker sees** unique animals in the desert.
- The **hikers see** unique animals in the desert.

 © Shell Education

NAME: ______________________ **DATE:** ______________

Directions: Use the symbol to cross out each word that is spelled incorrectly. Then, write the corrected word above it.

1. A dessert biome gets less than 10 inches (25.4 centimeters) of rainfall a year.

2. Animals lives in hot deserts and cold deserts.

3. Sandstormes are common in large, dusty deserts and can bother the animals.

4. Animals have different weighs to survive the extreme conditions of the desert.

5. Lizards, small rodents, snakes, and camels are sum of the animals that live in a desert.

Boost Your Learning!

When you come across a misspelled word that you don't know how to spell, circle it and write *sp* above the circle.

sp
Example: There are (byms) everywhere.

If you do know how to spell the word, delete it and write the word correctly above it.

biomes
Example: There are ~~byms~~ everywhere.

Editing
Desert Animals

NAME: ____________________ **DATE:** ____________________

Directions: Read the paragraph. Check for subject-verb agreement. Then, answer the question.

Desert animals must adapt to extreme heat and lack of water. Several animals is active only at night because of the daytime heat. Some animals don't need to drinks any water. They get enough from the plants and seeds they eat. Several desert animals do not have sweat glands, allowing them to holds in more moisture throughout the day. Birds have feathers to help keep them cool and covered during the day. Without adaptations, desert animals may not survive.

1. What makes this paragraph a strong informative/explanatory paragraph?

____

____

____

This week I learned:

- how to write proper subject-verb agreements
- how to correct misspelled words

NAME: ______________________ **DATE:** ______________

Directions: Place check marks in the circles with information that you would include in an informative/explanatory paragraph about animals in the tundra.

Tundra Animal Facts

- They have minimal skin exposure to stay warm.
- These animals either hibernate or migrate for the winter.
- The largest tundra animal is the polar bear.
- There are about 48 different animals in the tundra.
- There is always a fluctuation in population.
- They have adaptations for survival.

NAME: ______________________ DATE: ________________

Directions: Describe the types of animals that live in a tundra. Include specific facts about how the animals adapt and live in the environment. Use the facts on page 19 to help you draft your informative/explanatory paragraph.

Remember!

A strong informative/explanatory paragraph should include:

- a topic sentence
- details to support the main idea
- a concluding sentence

Printing Practice

Directions: Use your best printing to write two words from your paragraph.

 © Shell Education

NAME: ______________________ DATE: ________________

Directions: Write four complete sentences using one subject and one verb from the chart below in each sentence. Think about subject-verb agreement when choosing a subject and a verb.

Subjects	Verbs
polar bear	grow
arctic foxes	hibernates
squirrel	eats
shrubs	adapt
birds	migrate

1. ____

2. ____

3. ____

4. ____

Time to Improve!

Go back to the draft you wrote on page 20. Check to make sure that all of your sentences have subject-verb agreement.

NAME: ______________________ **DATE:** ______________

Directions: Read the sentences. Each one has a spelling error. Use the symbol to cross out the misspelled word. Then, write the correctly spelled word above it.

1. A polar bear's paw is vary large.
2. The squirrels' tales are very bushy.
3. The sun's rayz are shining brightly on the animals.
4. Most animals rely on their fat and long fur four warmth.

Remember!

You must always reread your writing to make sure you spell the words correctly.

Time to Improve!

Go back to the draft you wrote on page 20. Check to make sure that you have spelled all of your words correctly.

 © Shell Education

NAME: ______________________ **DATE:** ____________________

Directions: Describe the types of animals that live in a tundra. Include specific facts about how the animals adapt and live in the environment.

NAME: ______________________ **DATE:** ________________

Directions: Decide whether each activity is related to summer or fall. Write *S* for *summer* and *F* for *fall* next to the appropriate phrases.

_____ **1.** raking leaves

_____ **2.** carving pumpkins

_____ **3.** going to the beach

_____ **4.** cool weather

_____ **5.** taking a break from school

_____ **6.** long, hot days

_____ **7.** many crops are harvested

_____ **8.** taking vacations

 © Shell Education

NAME: ____________________ **DATE:** ____________________

Directions: Read the opinion paragraph. Circle the sentence that states the author's opinion. Then, underline parts that support the opinion.

Summer is the best time of the year. School is out, and there are so many fun things to do. Going to the beach, taking swimming lessons, and going on vacation are some of my favorites. Too bad it's not summer all year long. Chuck, the dog, also enjoys summer because there's more time for us to play with him. He loves going to the dog park, playing fetch, and swimming in the pool. Unfortunately, summer doesn't last forever.

Remember!

An opinion states a feeling or thought.

Example: Being able to play in the snow makes winter the best season.

Printing Practice abc

Directions: Use your best printing to write one adjective related to summer and one adjective related to fall activities.

____________________ ____________________

NAME: ______________________ **DATE:** ______________

Directions: Revise the underlined words in each sentence by writing the past-tense verb that can replace the underlined words.

1. Sara will learn how to rake the leaves.

   ____

2. He will carve the pumpkin on Saturday.

   ____

3. The children will go to the beach with their parents.

   ____

4. Ben will play with his beach ball at the pool.

   ____

Boost Your Learning!

In your writing, make sure that all of your verbs have the same tense. For example, if you are writing about something in the past, all of your verbs should be in past tense.

© Shell Education

NAME: ______________________ **DATE:** ______________

Directions: Use the ∧ symbol to place missing series commas in the paragraph.
Hint: There are four missing commas.

Summer is the best time of the year. School is out, and there are so many fun things to do. Going to the beach taking swimming lessons and going on vacation are some of my favorites. Too bad it's not summer all year long. Chuck, the dog, also enjoys summer because there's more time for us to play with him. He loves going to the dog park playing fetch and swimming in the pool. Unfortunately, summer doesn't last forever.

Boost Your Learning!

Series commas are used to separate a list of two or more things.

Example: The girls enjoy playing in the leaves∧, flying kites∧, and carving pumpkins.

NAME: ____________________ DATE: ____________

Directions: Read the opinion paragraph. Then, answer the questions.

Fall is the perfect season for enjoying the great outdoors. My favorite activity is hiking the nearby trails with my dog. I spend a lot of time at different parks throughout the fall season. I also like to play soccer after school with my friends. I think it's the perfect pastime for when the weather starts to cool off.

1. How do you know what the author's opinion is?

____

____

____

2. Explain how the author supports his or her opinion.

____

____

____

This week I learned:

- to use correct verb tenses
- to use series commas

 © Shell Education

NAME: ______________________ DATE: ________________

Directions: Draw a winter scene and a spring scene. Then, write three opinions about each season on the lines provided.

Winter	Spring
1. ______________	1. ______________
2. ______________	2. ______________
3. ______________	3. ______________

NAME: ______________________ **DATE:** ________________

Directions: It's a contest! Winter and spring both think they're the better season. Which season will you support? Provide reasons to support your opinion. Use your notes from page 29 to help draft your opinion paragraph.

Remember!

A strong opinion paragraph:

- has an introductory and a concluding sentence stating an opinion
- gives reasons that support the opinion

Printing Practice

Directions: Use your best printing to write two adjectives describing spring and two adjectives describing winter.

© Shell Education

NAME: ______________________ **DATE:** ______________

Directions: Use the present-tense verbs in the Word Bank to complete the sentences.

Word Bank

drive plants fall hatch wear

1. Billy ____________________ new flowers in the garden.
2. The leaves ____________________ from the tree because of the strong winter winds.
3. All of the children ____________________ heavy coats when they build snowmen.
4. The baby birds ____________________ out of the eggs in the nest.
5. Cars need chains as they ____________________ up the mountain roads.

Time to Improve!

Go back to the draft you wrote on page 30. Check to make sure that you have used the correct verb tenses in your writing.

NAME: ______________________ **DATE:** ________________

Directions: Use the ∧ symbol to place missing series commas in the sentences.

1. I like to ski snowboard and build snowmen in the winter.
2. There's snow rocks and ice everywhere!
3. Flowers trees and bushes begin to bloom in the springtime.
4. You can see butterflies birds and bees flying around the garden.

Remember!

Add series commas when three or more things are listed in a sentence.

Example: It is fun to have picnics∧, go swimming∧, and run at the park in spring.

Time to Improve!

Go back to the draft you wrote on page 30. Check to see if you list more than three things in your sentences. If you do, make sure you have series commas.

 © Shell Education

NAME: ______________________ **DATE:** ________________

Directions: Read the paragraph. Underline the opinion statements within the paragraph.

Wolves are excellent hunters and can be found all over the world. Most wolves weigh about 88 pounds (40 kilograms), but the heaviest wolves weigh over 176 pounds (80 kilograms). Wolves hunt and live in groups called packs. Their ability to work together is astounding. Wolves who hunt in the Arctic have to travel longer distances than those in the forest. Individual wolves hunt smaller animals such as squirrels, hares, or chipmunks, but a pack of wolves can hunt much larger animals such as caribou, moose, and yaks.

Printing Practice abc

Directions: Use your best printing to write the names of two wild animals.

____

____

NAME: ______________________ **DATE:** ________________

Directions: Underline the correct adjectives to complete the sentences.

1. Elephants are (bigger **or** biggest) than skunks.
2. Giraffes are the (taller **or** tallest) wild animals in existence.
3. Gorillas are (stronger **or** strongest) than the monkeys.
4. Cheetahs are the (faster **or** fastest) running land animal.
5. Wolves are (fiercer **or** fiercest) than dogs.

Boost Your Learning!

Comparative adjectives are used to compare two things. **Superlative adjectives** are used to compare more than two things.

Examples

- Lions are bigger than hyenas. (*comparative*)
- Ostriches lay the largest eggs of any type of bird. (*superlative*)

 © Shell Education

NAME: ______________________ **DATE:** ________________

Directions: Use the ≡ symbol to correct capitalization errors in the paragraph.

some of the greatest wild animals are in the ocean. dolphins, whales, and sharks are just a few examples. there are also thousands of different fish. ocean animals may be found anywhere from the pacific ocean to the atlantic ocean and beyond. their characteristics are quite different from those of land animals.

Boost Your Learning!

First words in sentences and proper nouns should always be capitalized.

Example: i love dolphins.
≡

NAME: ______________________ **DATE:** ________________

Directions: Reread the paragraph about wolves. Then, answer the question.

Wolves are excellent hunters and can be found all over the world. Most wolves weigh about 88 pounds (40 kilograms), but the heaviest wolves weigh over 176 pounds (80 kilograms). Wolves hunt and live in groups called packs. Their ability to work together is astounding. Wolves who hunt in the Arctic have to travel longer distances than those in the forest. Individual wolves hunt smaller animals such as squirrels, hares, or chipmunks, but a pack of wolves can hunt much larger animals such as caribou, moose, and yaks.

1. What evidence does the author provide to support his opinion that wolves are excellent hunters?

____

____

____

____

This week I learned:

- how to write opinions
- how to use comparative and superlative adjectives
- how to capitalize appropriate words

 © Shell Education

NAME: ______________________ **DATE:** ________________

Directions: Some animals are wild. Other animals are pets. What makes an animal a pet? Write the characteristics of pets in the outer bubbles.

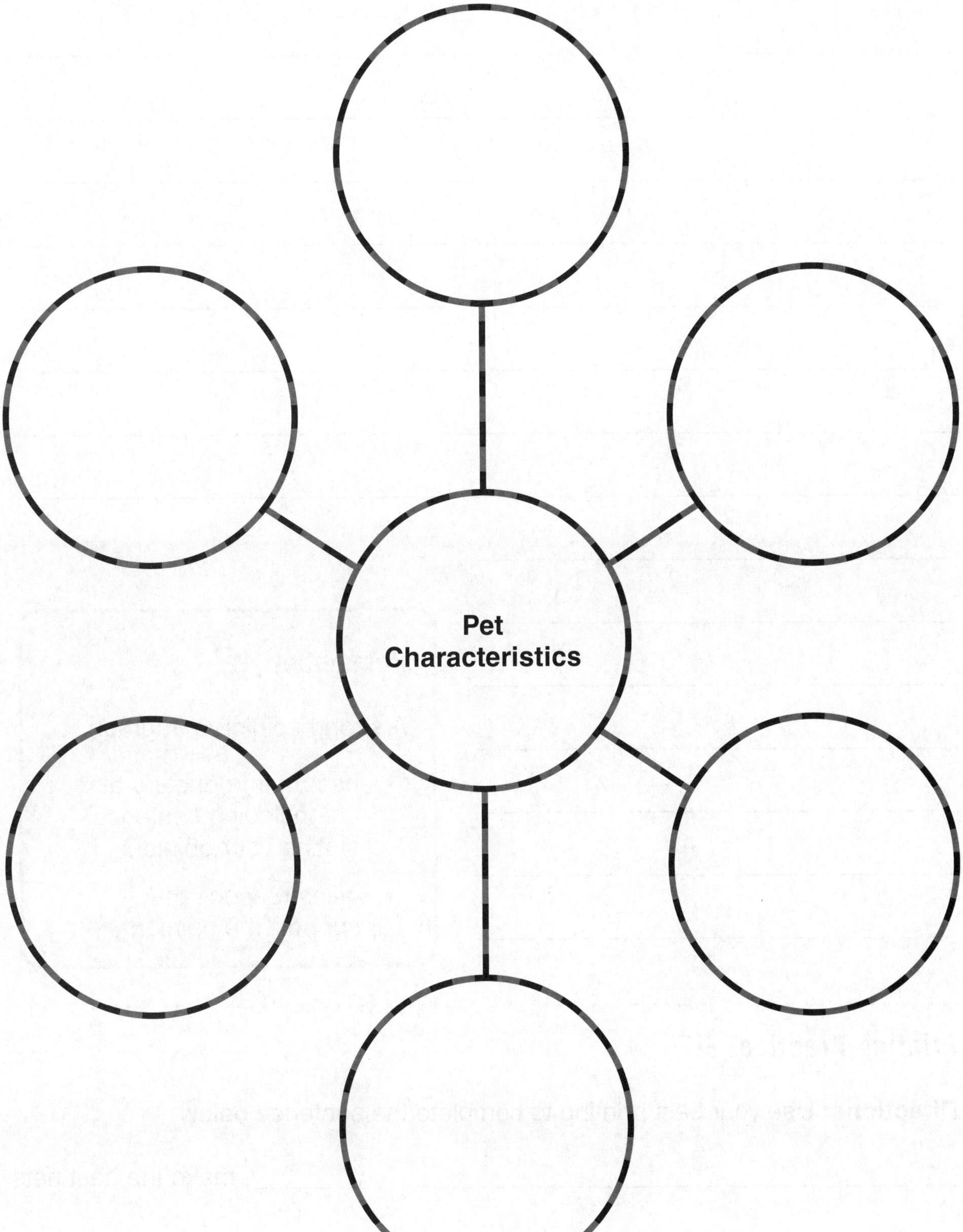

NAME: ______________________ **DATE:** ________________

Directions: Draft an opinion paragraph about which animal you think makes the best pet. Be sure to include descriptive adjectives to help support your opinion. Use the notes from page 39 to help you draft your paragraph.

Remember!

A strong opinion paragraph:

- has an introductory and a concluding sentence stating your opinion
- gives reasons that support the opinion

Printing Practice abc

Directions: Use your best printing to complete the sentence below.

______________________________ make the best pets.

 © Shell Education

NAME: ______________________ **DATE:** ________________

Directions: Read the original sentence. Think about how you can make it more interesting. Write a list of adjectives about rabbits. Then, use some of your adjectives to write a new and improved sentence.

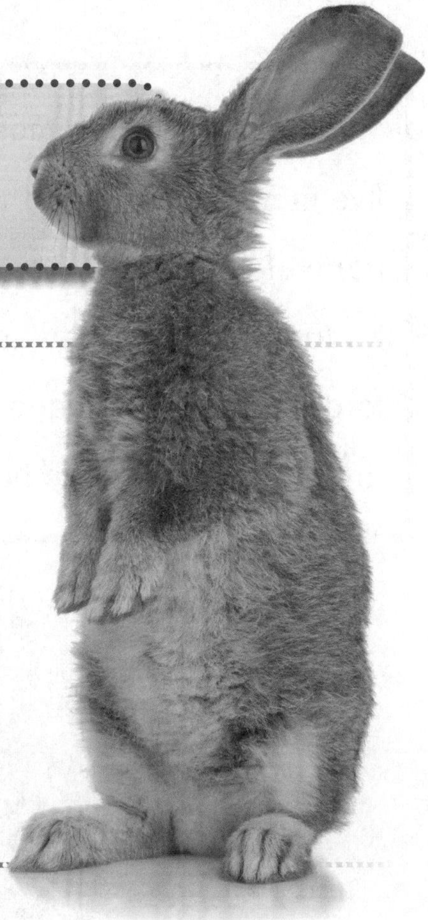

Original Sentence

Rabbits have ears.

Adjectives about Rabbits

- ✓ ______________________
- ✓ ______________________
- ✓ ______________________
- ✓ ______________________
- ✓ ______________________

My New and Improved Sentence

____

____

Boost Your Learning!

Want to spruce up your writing? Then use adjectives! **Adjectives** are words that describe nouns. They can make boring writing soar!

Time to Improve!

Go back to the draft you wrote on page 40. Can any of your sentences be improved? If you think they can, add adjectives to make them better.

NAME: ______________________ **DATE:** ______________

Directions: Read the paragraph. Use the ≡ symbol to correct the capitalization errors.

hamsters are the most amazing pets. They are small and cute. they live in cages and need very little food and water. hamsters can fit in the palm of your hand. They like to play with toys in their cages and can be fun to watch. they are fairly inexpensive to maintain, too. just don't forget to close the cage or else there might be a surprise scampering around the house the next day!

Remember!

The first words in sentences should always be capitalized.

Time to Improve!

Go back to the draft you wrote on page 40. Check to make sure that you capitalized your words correctly. If you didn't, correct them!

NAME: ______________________ **DATE:** ______________

Directions: Write an opinion paragraph about which animal you think makes the best pet. Be sure to include descriptive adjectives to help support your opinion.

NAME: ______________________ DATE: ______________

Directions: Read the sentences about four of our seven continents. Write *O* if the sentence is an opinion and *F* if it is a fact.

Antarctica

_____ It is the coldest place on Earth.

_____ I really enjoy playing in the snow.

_____ Many scientists work in Antarctica.

_____ Penguins, whales, and seals can be found there.

North America

_____ It has the lowest point on the continent, Death Valley, which is below sea level.

_____ It is the third-largest continent.

_____ The 50 states are all very interesting.

_____ It has every type of climate.

Africa

_____ The variety of wild animals you see on a safari is very cool.

_____ It is the second-largest continent.

_____ It has the longest river on Earth, the Nile River.

_____ The largest desert, the Sahara Desert, is located in Africa.

Asia

_____ It is the largest continent on Earth.

_____ I really like the traditions that Asian countries celebrate.

_____ It has the highest population rate.

_____ Asia contains 48 countries in it, including India and Thailand.

 © Shell Education

NAME: ______________________ **DATE:** ________________

Directions: Read the paragraph. Underline the adjectives. Then, answer the question.

Africa is the second-largest continent and home of the longest river, the Nile River. It is home to the Sahara Desert, the largest desert in the world. Africa has a hot climate throughout the year and is quite rich in minerals.

1. How do adjectives add to the paragraph?

____

____

____

Printing Practice abc

Directions: Use your best printing to write the names of two continents.

____

____

NAME: ______________________ DATE: ______________

Directions: The sentences are incomplete. Revise them so that they have complete subjects and predicates.

1. Soccer dominant game in South America.

____

____

2. Tree frogs, hedgehogs, and wild boars major animals in Europe.

____

____

3. Mr. Scientist said that Antarctica coldest place on Earth.

____

____

Boost Your Learning!

A complete sentence needs a subject and a predicate. The **subject** is who or what the sentence is about. The **predicate** is what happens.

Example: Antarctica (subject) is very large. (predicate)

© Shell Education

NAME: ______________________________ **DATE:** ____________________

Directions: Read the paragraph. Use the ⌒ symbol to correct the spelling errors. **Hint:** There are seven spelling errors.

It is believed that in the passed, all continents were once joyned together. This area eventually broke apart, and now we have seven continents. Sum are completely surrounded by water, and othurs are connected to each other. Some continents have many countrys, while others have only a few. Research has shown that continents are still moveing, witch is called continental drift.

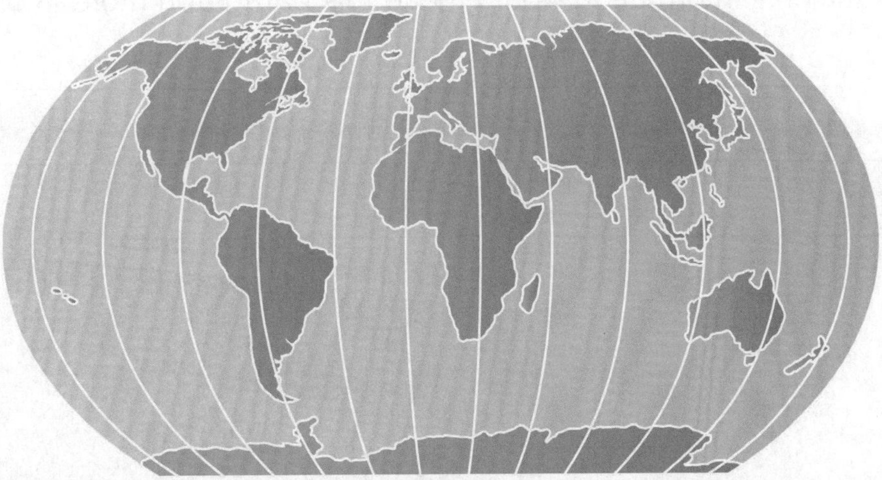

Remember!

When you come across a misspelled word that you don't know how to spell, circle it and write *sp* above the circle.

sp
Example: There are sevn continents.

If you do know how to spell the word, delete it and write the word correctly above it.

seven
Example: There are sevn continents.

NAME: ____________________ **DATE:** ____________

Publishing
Continents

Directions: Reread the paragraph. Then, answer the questions.

Africa is the second-largest continent and home of the longest river, the Nile River. It is home to the Sahara Desert, the largest desert in the world. Africa has a hot climate throughout the year and is quite rich in minerals.

1. What makes this paragraph an informative/explanatory paragraph?

____

____

____

2. What additional information would make this paragraph more informative?

____

____

____

This week I learned:

- how to identify adjectives
- how to use subject pronouns
- how to identify spelling errors

 © Shell Education

NAME: ______________________ **DATE:** ______________

Directions: Look at the list of bodies of water on the left. Draw sketches of them. Then, add a few things you know about each one.

Bodies of Water	Sketches	Information about Bodies of Water
river		
pond		
ocean		
lake		

Drafting
Bodies of Water

NAME: ______________________ **DATE:** ______________

Directions: Draft an informative/explanatory paragraph about bodies of water. Include at least two types of bodies of water, and explain what each one looks like. Use your notes from page 49 to help draft your pargraph.

Remember!

A strong informative/explanatory paragraph should include:

- a topic sentence
- details to support the main idea
- a concluding sentence

Printing Practice

Directions: Use your best printing to write the names of three types of bodies of water.

 © Shell Education

NAME: ____________________ **DATE:** ________________

Directions: Read the paragraph. Underline the sentences that are not complete. On the lines below, rewrite the sentences to make them complete.

The Atlantic Ocean is the second largest ocean on Earth. It is between the Americas, Europe, and Africa. Atlantic Ocean about half the size of Pacific Ocean. It covers about 20 percent of Earth's surface. The equator divides it into the North Pacific Ocean and the South Pacific Ocean. Many islands found within the Atlantic, including the Bahamas and Greenland. Common sea life includes sharks, the grey Atlantic seal, and the humpback whale.

1. ____

____

2. ____

____

Remember!

A complete sentence needs a subject and a predicate. The subject is who or what the sentence is about. The predicate is what happens.

Time to Improve!

Go back to the draft you wrote on page 50. Reread your writing to make sure that all of your sentences are complete. If they are not complete, revise them to make them correct.

NAME: ______________________ **DATE:** ______________

Editing

Bodies of Water

Directions: Use the ꝭ symbol to fix the misspelled words.

1. The smallest body of water is a creek, which is aslo known as a brook.
2. The Gulf of Mexico is olny partially enclosed by land.
3. A lake is a bdy of water completely surrounded by land.
4. The Mediterranean See is attached to the Atlantic Ocean.
5. Oceans are the larggest bodies of water on Earth.

Time to Improve!

Go back to the draft you wrote on page 50. Check to make sure that you have spelled all of the words correctly.

© Shell Education

NAME: ______________________ **DATE:** ____________________

Directions: Write an informative/explanatory paragraph about bodies of water. Include at least two types of bodies of water, and explain what each one looks like.

____

____

____

____

____

____

____

____

____

____

____

NAME: ______________________ **DATE:** ________________

Directions: Draw a picture of your favorite birthday celebration or your dream birthday. Then, write two sentences describing it.

____

____

____

____

 © Shell Education

NAME: ______________________ **DATE:** ________________

Directions: Circle prefixes or suffixes in the underlined words. Then, answer the question.

It was Sara's ninth birthday. She was anxiously waiting for all her friends to arrive. Her mother was busy carefully decorating the house, as she didn't want to have to redo anything later. Her dad put their dog inside the garage because he usually misbehaves around a lot of people. The time had come; it was one o'clock and guests had started to arrive. Sara was ready for an eventful day with her friends.

1. How do the underlined words add to the paragraph?

____

____

____

Printing Practice abc

Directions: Write the name of the month you were born in using good printing.

____

Boost Your Learning!

A **suffix** is a letter or group of letters added to the end of a word. A **prefix** is a small word added to the beginning of a base word. Both slightly change words' meanings.

Examples

- Suffixes: friend ⟶ friend**ly** hot ⟶ hott**er**
- Prefixes: guide ⟶ **mis**guide game ⟶ **pre**game

NAME: ______________________ DATE: ____________

Revising
Birthdays

Directions: Use the adverbs from the Word Bank to replace the underlined phrases.

Word Bank

extremely peacefully carefully swiftly happily

1. Mom and Dad politely disagreed on the birthday theme.

   ____

2. I needed to refill my cup of quickly.

   ____

3. My teacher carefully wished me a happy birthday.

   ____

4. We had to be really cautious while swinging the bat at the piñata.

   ____

5. My parents cautiously drove away from the party.

   ____

Boost Your Learning!

Adverbs modify verbs. They help add detail to the text. They may be placed before or after verbs.

Example:

- Billy laughed hysterically at the clown's joke.
- Billy hysterically laughed at the clown's joke.

© Shell Education

NAME: ______________________ **DATE:** ________________

Directions: Use the ∨ symbol to add quotation marks to the sentences.

1. Listen up! It's time to cut the cake said Jacob's mom.

2. This bounce house is so much fun! cried Sam.

3. Jacob's mom said Don't forget your goodie bags!

4. This chocolate cake is delicious I said.

Boost Your Learning!

Here are a few tips for using **quotation marks:**

- Quotation marks go before and after the words people say.
- The quotation starts with a capital letter.
- If the quote comes before the person who said it, put a comma between the last word and ending quotation mark.

Example: "Yosemite National Park is in California," the teacher explained.

- If the quote comes after the person who said it, put a comma between the person who spoke and the beginning quotation mark.

Example: The boy said, "I would like to visit Yosemite someday."

Publishing
Birthdays

NAME: ______________________________ **DATE:** ____________________

Directions: Read the narrative. The sentences are out of order. Number them so that they are in the correct order. Then, rewrite the paragraph using the correct order.

_____Sara was so excited for her birthday party. _____Lastly, everyone munched on some delicious chocolate cake. _____Then came several friends and a few more family members. _____First, they played games, and musical chairs was the favorite. _____Sara enjoyed opening her gifts next. _____Her grandparents were the first to arrive.

This week I learned:

- how to identify prefixes and suffixes
- how to use adverbs

© Shell Education

NAME: ______________________ **DATE:** ________________

Directions: Think about a time you celebrated a holiday. Write the name of the holiday in the center circle. Then, write notes about the event in the outer circles, including whom you celebrated with and what happened.

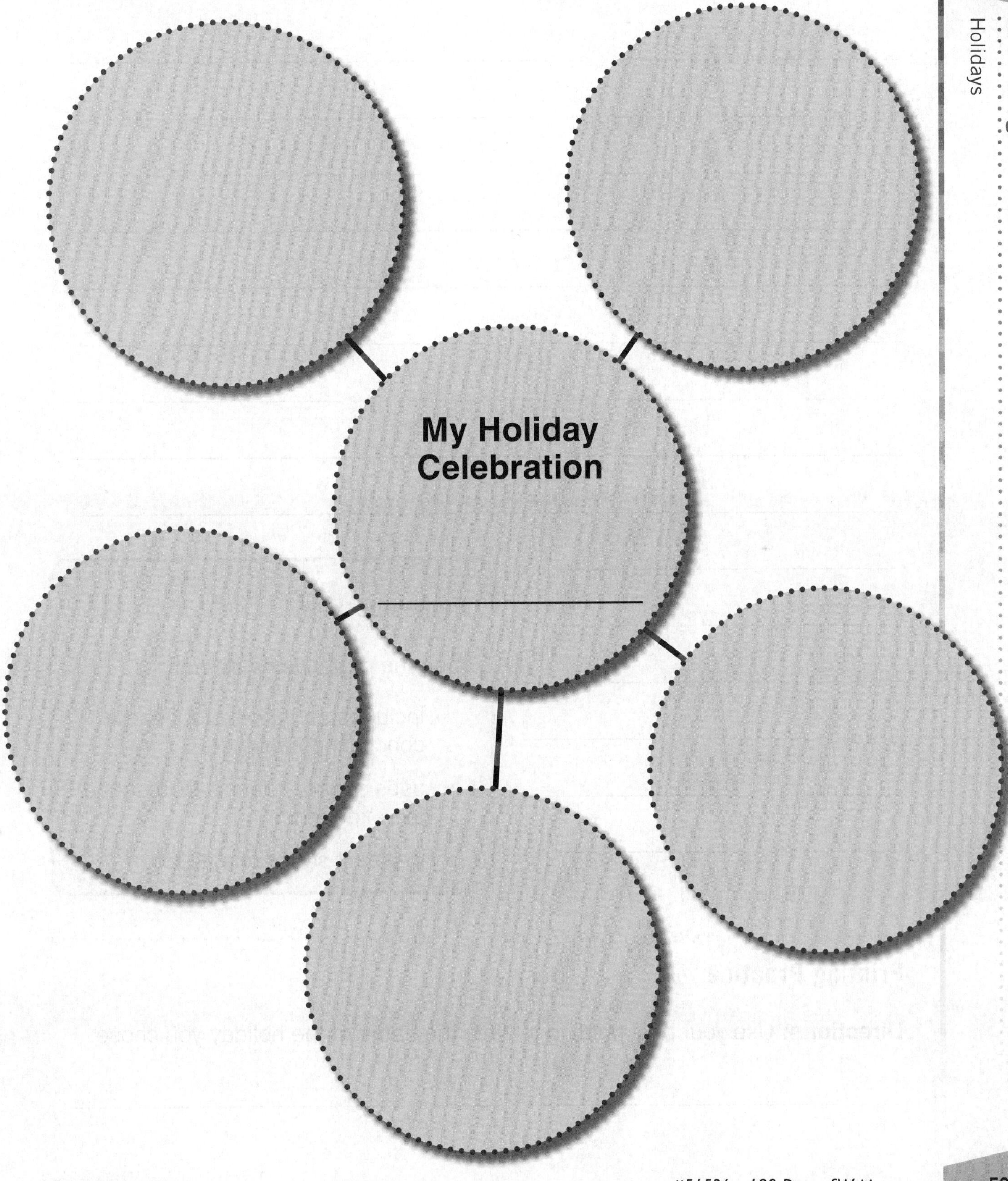

NAME: ______________________ **DATE:** ______________

Directions: Think about a holiday you have celebrated. Describe the celebration. Include at least two lines of dialogue.

Remember!

A strong narrative paragraph:

- includes an introductory and a concluding sentence
- uses sensory details to describe the experience
- makes it sound like a story

Printing Practice abc

Directions: Use your best printing to write the name of the holiday you chose.

 © Shell Education

NAME: ______________________ **DATE:** ______________

Directions: Use the chart below to write four sentences about holidays. Use each holiday and adverb only once.

Holiday	Adverb
Halloween	quietly
Hanukkah	peacefully
Chinese New Year	happily
Valentine's Day	cheerfully

1. ______________________________

2. ______________________________

3. ______________________________

4. ______________________________

Time to Improve!

Go back to the draft you wrote on page 60. Did you use any adverbs in your writing? If so, make sure that you used them correctly. If not, try to add some!

NAME: ______________________ **DATE:** ______________

Directions: Use the ∨ symbol to add quotation marks to the narrative paragraph.

My favorite thing about the holidays is celebrating with my family. When it's time to eat, my mom calls down, Olivia, it's time for the feast.

I respond with, Hooray, I'm coming right now!

I love baking special recipes with my grandma and singing traditional songs with my family that comes to visit from all over the country. We enjoy homemade dessert each night as we sit around and share memories from the past year. My grandmother repeatedly says, It's just so great to see you. I've missed you!

My family members call out, We've missed you, too, Grandmother. Now let's make the best of it!

She's not the only one who feels this way. I find myself thinking the same thing as I soak in the time with my loved ones.

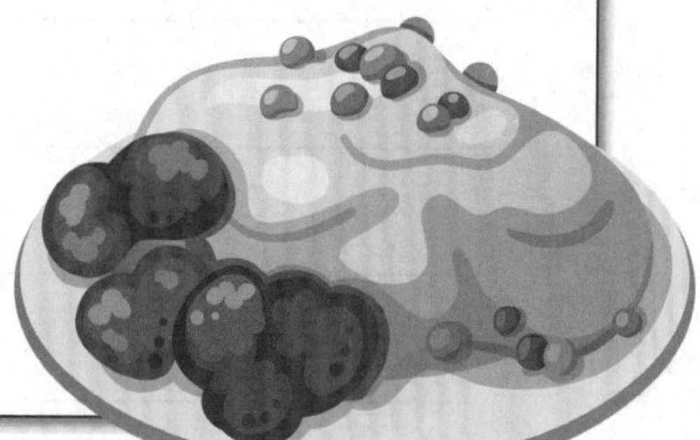

Boost Your Learning!

When you include dialogue in your writing, you must always begin a new line when a new speaker is speaking.

Time to Improve!

Go back to the draft you wrote on page 60. Check to make sure you used quotation marks correctly. If you don't have any in your writing, try to add some new lines.

 © Shell Education

NAME: ______________________ **DATE:** ________________

Directions: Think about a holiday you have celebrated. Describe the celebration. Include at least two lines of dialogue.

Prewriting
Tornadoes

NAME: ______________________ **DATE:** ______________

Directions: What do you know about tornadoes? Place check marks in the bubbles with adjectives that best describe tornadoes.

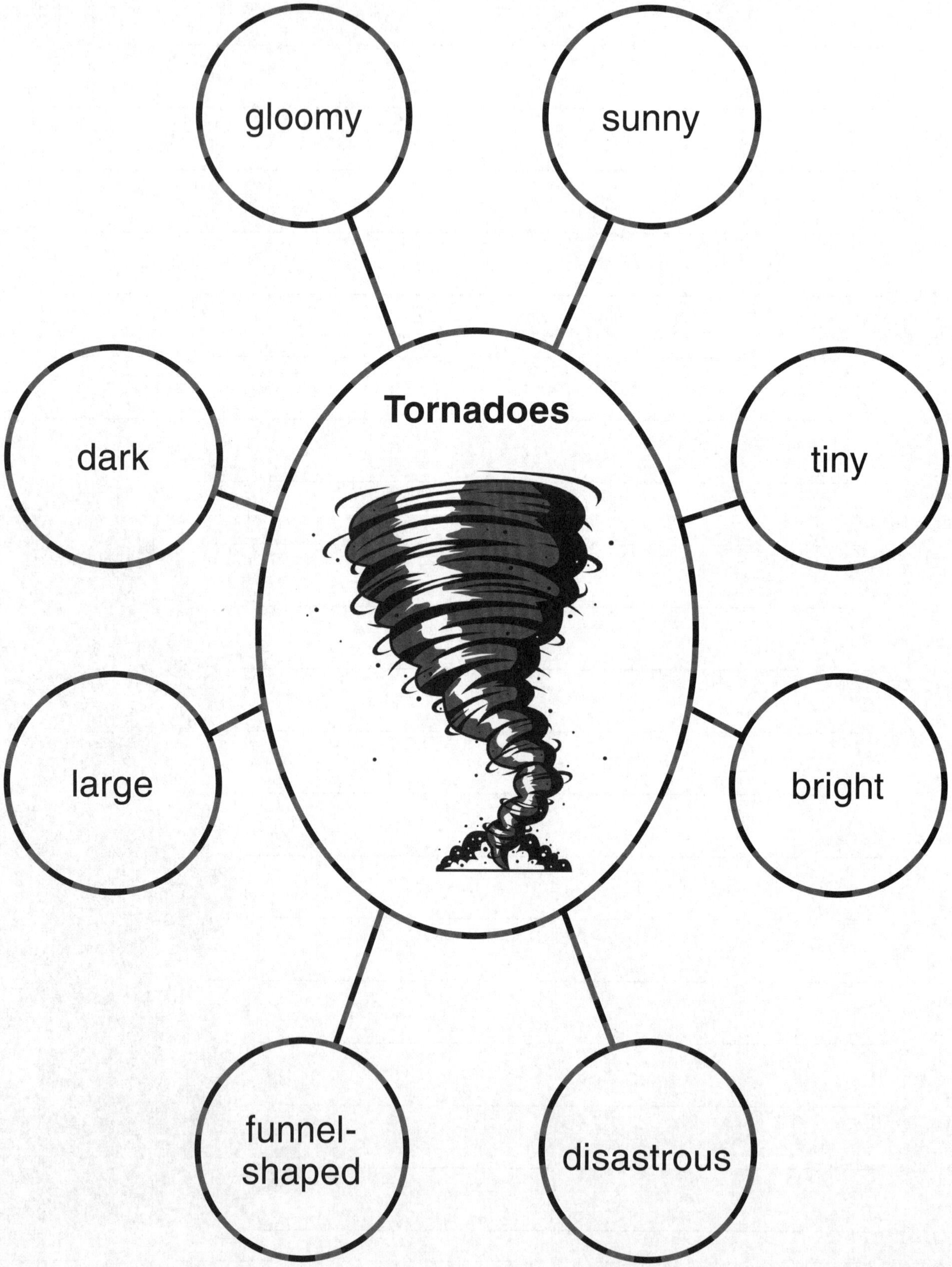

NAME: ______________________ **DATE:** ________________

Directions: Use context clues and words from the Word Bank to complete the sentences.

Word Bank

rapidly miles twisters rotate tornadoes

Tornadoes are sometimes called ________________.

They are ________________ spinning tubes of air.

Most tornadoes travel a few ________________.

In the northern hemisphere, tornadoes usually

________________ in a counterclockwise direction. The

United States has more ________________ than any

other country.

Printing Practice abc

Directions: How do you think you'd feel if you were near a tornado? Write that word in your best printing.

____

Revising · Tornadoes

NAME: ______________________ **DATE:** ______________

Directions: Underline the subject and circle the verb in each sentence. Check for subject-verb agreement. On the lines below, write the corrected sentences. If there are no mistakes, write *Correct as is*. The first one is done for you.

1. A tornado causes a lot of damage.

   Correct as is

2. The airs whirls upward.

   ____

3. A tornado moves across the land.

   ____

4. A tornado touch the ground.

   ____

 © Shell Education

NAME: ______________________ **DATE:** ________________

Directions: Use the ≡ symbol to correct any capitalization mistakes within the paragraph. **Hint:** There are six mistakes.

sometimes, a funnel cloud can be mistaken for a tornado. A funnel cloud is a cone-shaped cloud that doesn't touch the ground. a tornado happens when a funnel cloud reaches the ground. kansas, oklahoma, and texas are common areas for tornadoes to occur. They usually happen in the spring and summer months and can sometimes bring hail. tornadoes are destructive yet fascinating natural disasters.

Quick Practice

Directions: Circle the adjectives in the sentences.

1. The huge, gray tornado zoomed across the empty farm.

2. There are about fifty tornadoes a year in the central part of the United States.

Publishing
Tornadoes

NAME: ______________________ **DATE:** ______________

Directions: Reread the paragraph about tornadoes. Think about how you can improve the paragraph based on what you have learned this week. Then, rewrite the new-and-improved paragraph below.

Tornadoes are sometimes called twisters. They are rapidly spinning tubes of air. Most travel for a few miles. In the northern hemisphere, tornadoes usually rotate in a counterclockwise direction. The United States has more tornadoes than any other country.

____

____

____

____

____

____

____

____

Boost Your Learning!

A strong paragraph has an introductory sentence, strong details, and a concluding sentence.

This week I learned:

- how to use adjectives
- how to use context clues
- how to use proper subject-verb agreement
- how to fix capitalization errors

 © Shell Education

NAME: ______________________ DATE: ________________

Directions: Read the statements about earthquakes. Write *F* if the statement is a fact. Write *O* if the statement is an opinion.

_____ **1.** About 50,000 earthquakes happen every year.

_____ **2.** I get scared during earthquakes.

_____ **3.** It's important to have a safety plan for when an earthquake hits.

_____ **4.** Most earthquakes go unnoticed.

_____ **5.** Sometimes, aftershocks happen after a big earthquake hits.

_____ **6.** Scientists measure the magnitude of earthquakes with seismometers.

_____ **7.** People prefer to have earthquakes at night.

_____ **8.** Earth's moving plates are what cause earthquakes.

NAME: ______________________ DATE: ______________

Drafting
Earthquakes

Directions: Think about earthquakes. Draft a paragraph about earthquakes. Include facts about how they begin and what destruction they can cause. Use the facts from page 69 to help draft your informative/explanatory paragraph.

Remember!

A strong informative/explanatory paragraph should include:

- a topic sentence
- details to support the main idea
- a concluding sentence

Printing Practice abc

Directions: Use your best printing to write the words *earthquake* and *fault*.

 © Shell Education

NAME: ______________________ **DATE:** ________________

Directions: Some of the sentences in the paragraph are incomplete. Use the subjects in the Word Bank to complete the paragraph.

Word Bank

Some earthquakes These plates Earth's crust

________________ is made of large areas of flat rock called tectonic plates. Where these plates meet is called a *fault*. ________________ move slowly, causing a tremble through the crust up to Earth's surface. ________________ are minor and cause little harm, while others are intense and cause great destruction. The center point of an earthquake is called the *epicenter*.

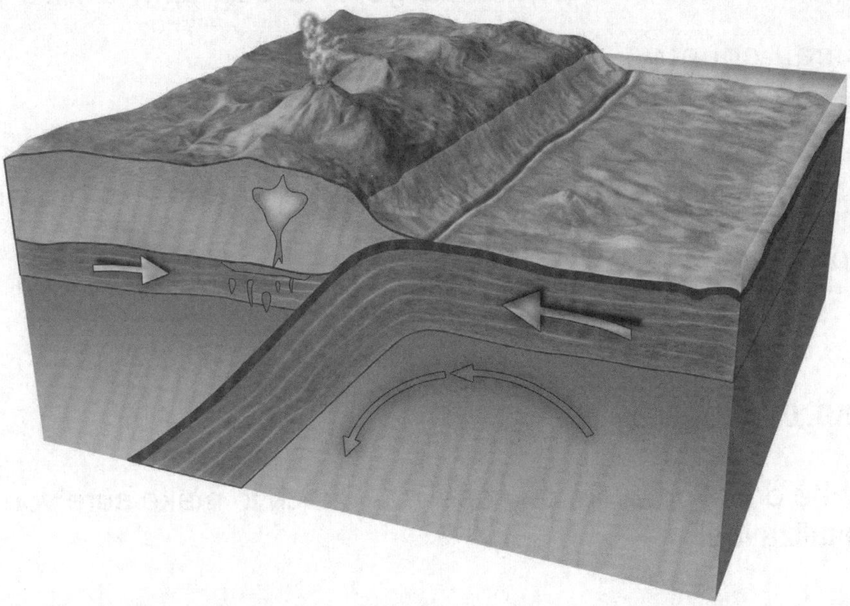

Time to Improve!

Go back to the draft you wrote on page 70. Check that all of your sentences are complete.

NAME: ______________________ **DATE:** ______________

Editing
Earthquakes

Directions: Use the ≡ and / symbols to correct the capitalization errors in the sentences.

1. The tectonic plates Shifted back and forth, causing a small earthquake.

2. An earthquake is sometimes quite Terrifying, and people panic.

3. mudslides are common after a large earthquake because the soil has shifted.

4. Great damage can come from the Tremendous force of an earthquake.

5. tsunami waves can be quite large and can ruin entire cities or a small country.

6. The amount of damage an Earthquake causes is based on its depth.

Time to Improve!

Go back to the draft you wrote on page 70. Check to make sure you used correct capitalization.

© Shell Education

NAME: ______________________ **DATE:** ____________________

Directions: Think about earthquakes. Write an informative/explanatory paragraph about earthquakes. Include facts about how they begin and what destruction they can cause.

____

____

____

____

____

____

____

____

____

____

____

____

NAME: ____________________ **DATE:** ____________________

Directions: Read the paragraphs about airplanes and helicopters. Then, fill in the Venn diagram with the similarities and differences between airplanes and helicopters.

Airplanes are used to transport people and things. Some people like to fly them for fun. An airplane's wings help lift the plane at takeoff. A pilot sits at the front of the plane, called a cockpit.

Helicopters lift off the ground vertically. They use spinning blades to help them with the takeoff. They can be used to transport and rescue people as well as to fight fires. Although they are noisy, they can fit in hard-to-reach places.

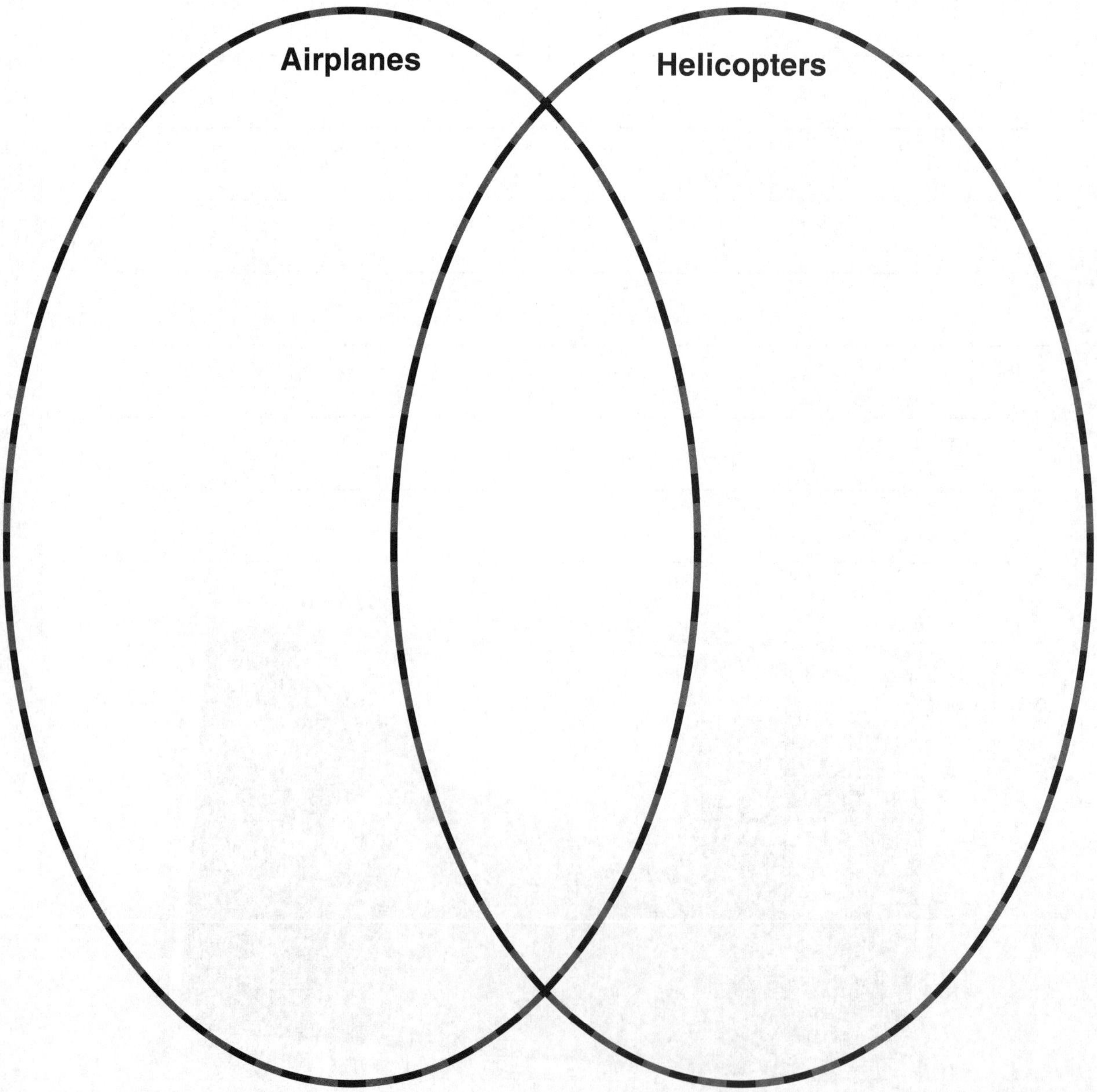

© Shell Education

NAME: ______________________ **DATE:** ________________

Directions: Complete the narrative paragraph by adding a concluding sentence.

Vince was anxious to board the plane. It was his first time on an airplane. He wondered how he would pass the time, as it was a three-hour flight to his grandmother's hometown. He had puzzle books, a music player, and a book. Vince hoped for a smooth flight with no turbulence. The plane took off, and soon enough, they were well above the clouds. Vince's favorite part was the free drink and pretzel snacks handed out by the flight attendants. He rotated between doing his puzzles, listening to music, and reading his book. Before he knew it, the pilot was preparing to land the airplane.

____

____.

Printing Practice abc

Directions: Use your best printing to write the words *helicopter* and *airplane*.

____

____

Revising

Air Travel

NAME: ______________________ **DATE:** ________________

Directions: Rewrite the simple sentences to make compound sentences about helicopters.

Example

Simple Sentences: Sara is excited for her helicopter ride. Sara has never been in a helicopter.

Compound Sentence: Sara is excited for her helicopter ride because she has never been in a helicopter before.

1. Landon thinks helicopters are fascinating. They can hover motionless in the air.

____

____

____

2. They are very useful means of transportation. Officer Frank uses helicopters to help protect people.

____

____

____

 © Shell Education

NAME: ____________________ **DATE:** ________________

Directions: Use the ∧ symbol to add adverbs to the sentences.

1. The flight instructor told me to buckle up, listen up, and look up.

2. Dad saw hilltops, lakes, and hundreds of trees from up in the helicopter.

3. "The best part was hovering like a hummingbird," said Grandpa.

4. You can twist, turn, and dive in some planes.

Boost Your Learning!

Adverbs modify verbs and often end with the suffix *-ly*.

Example: The train moved quick**ly**.

NAME: ______________________ **DATE:** ______________

Directions: Reread the paragraph. In the margins, add notes where dialogue can be added to make the paragraph more interesting.

Vince was anxious to board the plane. It was his first time on an airplane. He wondered how he would pass the time, as it was a three-hour flight to his grandmother's hometown. He had puzzle books, a music player, and a book. Vince hoped for a smooth flight with no turbulence. The plane took off, and soon enough, they were well above the clouds. Vince's favorite part was the free drink and pretzel snacks handed out by the flight attendants. He rotated between doing his puzzles, listening to his music, and reading his book. Before he knew it, the pilot was preparing to land the airplane.

This week I learned:

- how to write compound sentences
- how to use adverbs
- how to write narratives

 © Shell Education

NAME: ______________________________ **DATE:** ____________________

Directions: Name four different types of land transportation. Then, write a sentence about each of them.

1. ____________________:

____

____

2. ____________________:

____

____

3. ____________________:

____

____

4. ____________________:

____

____

NAME: ______________________ **DATE:** ______________

Directions: Imagine traveling somewhere by land. Describe your experience. Be sure to include characters, setting, problem(s), rising action, and a solution.
Challenge: Include dialogue, too!

____

____

____

____

____

____

____

____

____

____

____

Remember!

A strong narrative paragraph:

- includes an introductory and a concluding sentence
- uses sensory details to describe the experience
- makes it sound like a story

Printing Practice

Directions: Use your best printing to complete the sentence.

I want to travel by ______________________ some day.

Boost Your Learning!

Use commas and quotation marks when writing dialogue. Also, when a new speaker is speaking, he or she needs a new line.

Example: Ryan said, "I don't like trains as much as I like motorcycles."

 © Shell Education

NAME: ______________________ **DATE:** ______________

Directions: Look at the picture. List as many verbs as you can about bicycle transportation. Then, write two compound sentences using those verbs.

- ______________________
- ______________________
- ______________________
- ______________________
- ______________________
- ______________________
- ______________________
- ______________________
- ______________________
- ______________________

1. ____

2. ____

Time to Improve!

Go back to the draft you wrote on page 80. Review all of the verbs. Try using different verbs to make your writing more exciting!

NAME: ______________________ **DATE:** ______________

Editing
Land Travel

Directions: Use the ∧ symbol to add adverbs that support the underlined words.

1. The paramedic drove to the hospital.

2. Bob spoke to the students about school bus safety.

3. The driver pulled over his truck, waiting for the storm to pass.

4. Sally watched the technician install new tires on her car.

5. After school, Carlos rode his skateboard home.

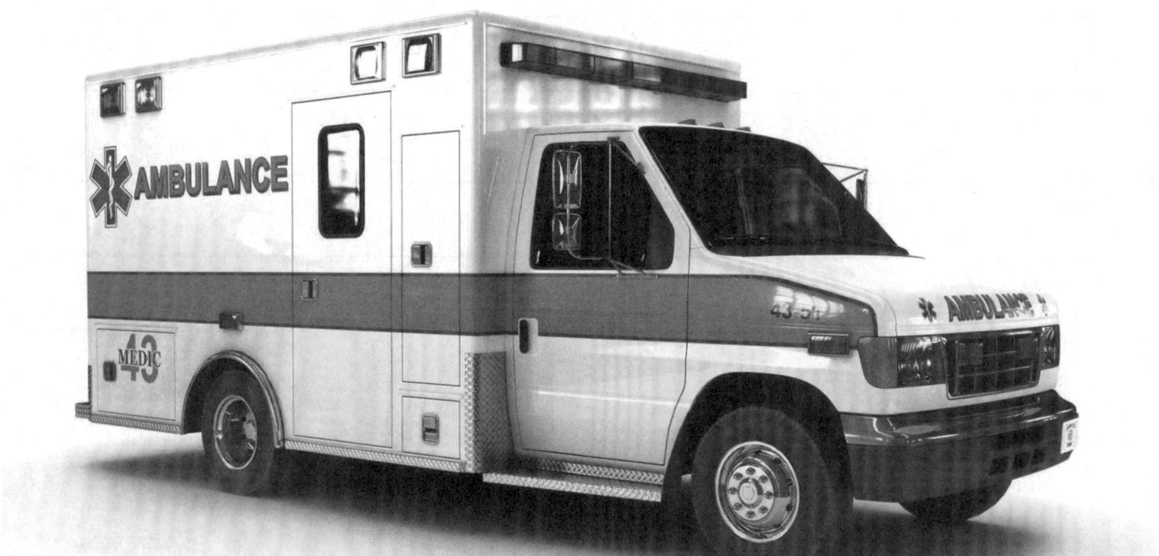

Remember!

Adverbs modify verbs and often end with the suffix *-ly*.

Example: The train moved quick**ly**.

Time to Improve!

Go back to the draft you wrote on page 80. Did you use adverbs in your writing? If so, make sure they support the verbs you used correctly.

NAME: ____________________ **DATE:** ____________________

Directions: Imagine traveling somewhere by land. Describe your experience. Be sure to include characters, setting, problem(s), rising action, and a solution.
Challenge: Include dialogue, too!

NAME: ______________________ **DATE:** ________________

Directions: Place check marks in the circles with character traits that you think superheroes should have.

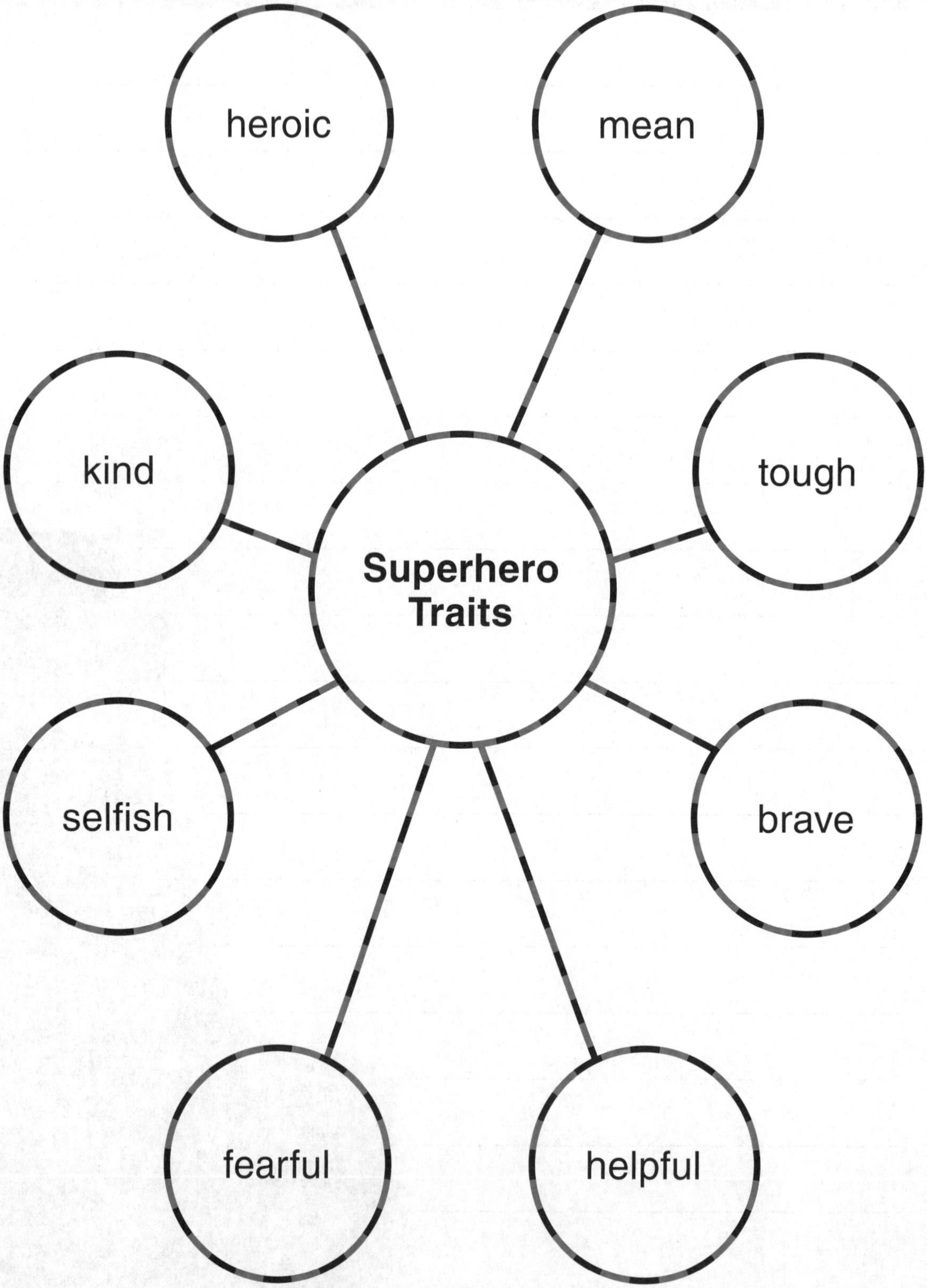

© Shell Education

NAME: ______________________ **DATE:** ________________

Directions: Read the paragraph. Underline the sentences that are not complete.

Are a great part of entertainment history. There are many different types of superheroes, each one having his or her own unique trait, or special power. Enjoy reading about superheroes. They embody a lifestyle unlike ours, making them quite interesting. They have also come to life over the years on movie screens for all ages to enjoy. Seeing a superhero in action on the big screen is a thrilling opportunity that all should experience at least once.

Printing Practice abc

Directions: Complete the sentence. Then, write your reason why.

My favorite superpower is ______________________________ .

____

____ .

NAME: ______________________ **DATE:** ______________

Directions: Rewrite the sentences to show possession.

1. The strength of a superhero is great.

____

____

2. The power of a superhero is the best part about him or her.

____

____

3. The battles of superheroes are always intense.

____

____

Remember!

You must use an apostrophe to show possession.

Quick Practice

Directions: Define the parts of speech.

1. A noun is ______________________________________

2. A verb shows ____________________________________

© Shell Education

NAME: ______________________ **DATE:** ______________

Directions: Use the symbol to change the verbs into present tense.

1. One superhero's power <u>was</u> the ability to fly.

2. A formula's radioactive elements <u>were</u> horrible because they <u>made</u> superheroes weak.

3. The sun's light <u>was</u> awesome because it <u>gave</u> superheroes additional powers.

4. The public's belief in superheroes <u>was</u> important.

5. A superhero <u>were</u> lucky to have his or her family's strong moral beliefs to look up to.

Boost Your Learning!

When you want to replace a word in a sentence, use this symbol. Then, write the correct word above it.

wish

Example: I wished I could meet a superhero.

NAME: ______________________ **DATE:** ________________

Directions: Reread the paragraph about superheroes. Then, answer the questions.

Superheroes are a great part of entertainment history. There are many different types of superheroes, each one having his or her own unique trait, or special power. Both adults and children enjoy reading about superheroes. They embody a lifestyle unlike ours, making them quite interesting. They have also come to life over the years on movie screens for all ages to enjoy. Seeing a superhero in action on the big screen is a thrilling experience that all should experience at least once.

1. What makes this an opinion paragraph?

____

____

____

____

2. Underline context clues that reveal opinions.

This week I learned:

- how to use present tense verbs
- how to write opinion paragraphs

 © Shell Education

NAME: ______________________________ **DATE:** ____________________

Directions: Place check marks in the circles that you think characterize villains.

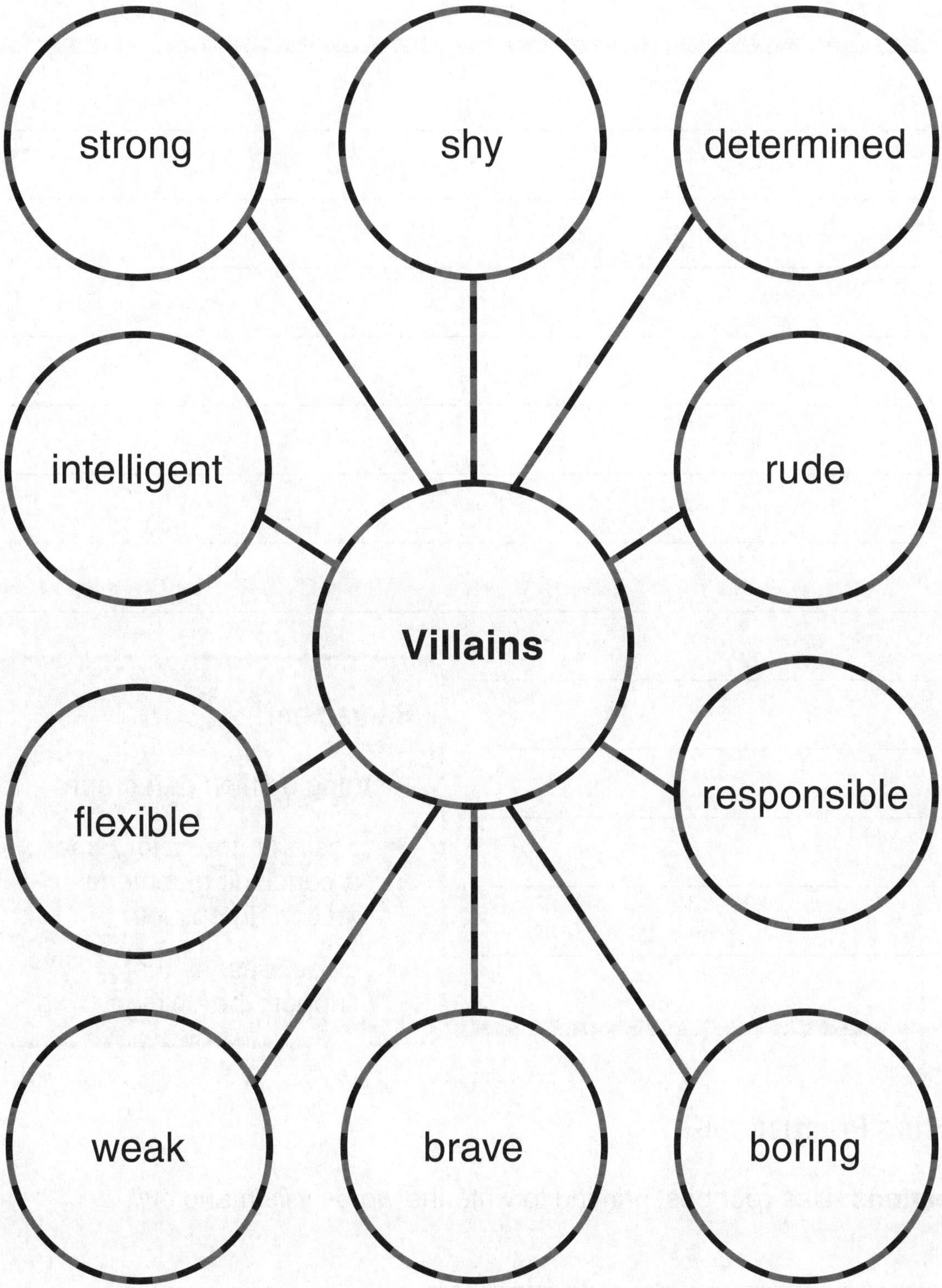

NAME: ______________________ **DATE:** ______________

Directions: Everyone seems to always root for superheroes. People think villains are too evil to support. Draft an opinion paragraph stating why we should understand villains' perspectives. Use your notes from page 89 to help draft your paragraph.

Remember!

A strong opinion paragraph:

- has an introductory and a concluding sentence stating an opinion
- gives reasons that support the opinion

Printing Practice abc

Directions: Use your best printing to write the words *villain* and *evil*.

 © Shell Education

Revising

Villains

NAME: ____________________ **DATE:** ________________

Directions: Rewrite the sentences to show possession.

1. The powers of a villain are evil.

2. It's wonderful that the enemies of villains defeat them.

3. It's interesting how the egos of villains can cause them to lose a battle.

4. The evil of a villain can be harmful to those around him or her.

Remember!

You must use an apostrophe to show possession.

Time to Improve!

Go back to the draft you wrote about villains on page 90. If you have included any possessive nouns in your writing, make sure you used apostrophes correctly.

NAME: ______________________________ **DATE:** ____________________

Directions: Read the paragraph. Use the symbol to correct any verbs that are not in the present tense. **Hint:** There are four errors.

Villains made great characters in comic books and movies. It is always interesting how evil they can be. Each one was unique. Sometimes, they are treated unfairly. Everyone usually roots for the superheroes. I thought people should understand more about the villains. If we know more about them, we might understand why they are the way they are. Maybe one day, superheroes and villains could got along.

Remember!

When you want to replace a word in a sentence, use this symbol . Then, write the correct word above it.

wish

Example: I ~~wished~~ I could meet a villain.

Time to Improve!

Go back to the draft you wrote on page 90. Did you use the correct tenses for the verbs? If not, correct them.

© Shell Education

NAME: ____________________ **DATE:** ______________

Directions: Everyone seems to always root for superheroes. People think villains are too evil to support. Write an opinion paragraph stating why we should understand villains' perspectives.

Prewriting
Grand Canyon

NAME: ______________________ **DATE:** ______________

Directions: Write *fact* or *opinion* next to each statement about the Grand Canyon.

1. The Grand Canyon is huge. ______________________
2. It is the most spectacular natural wonder. ______________________
3. The Grand Canyon has millions of visitors each year. ____________
4. It is made of red rock. ______________________
5. Everyone should find time to visit the Grand Canyon. ____________

 © Shell Education

NAME: ____________________ **DATE:** ______________

Directions: Read the paragraph about the Grand Canyon. Underline any incomplete sentences.

The Grand Canyon located in Arizona. It is 277 miles (446 kilometers) long. The Colorado River runs through the Grand Canyon. Have lived around the Grand Canyon for thousands of years. People enjoy visiting this beautiful place. Visitors often hike the canyon or go rafting in the river.

Printing Practice abc

Directions: Use your best printing to rewrite the sentence.

The Grand Canyon is a massive canyon of red rock.

____

____.

NAME: ______________________________ **DATE:** ____________________

Directions: Circle the correct adjective to make each sentence complete.

1. The air here is some of the (cleaner **or** cleanest) in the United States.
2. It is 4 miles (6 kilometers) wide at the (narrower **or** narrowest) point.
3. The Colca Canyon is (deeper **or** deepest) than the Grand Canyon.
4. The Grand Canyon is the (more **or** most) famous canyon in the world.
5. Its (wider **or** widest) point stretches 18 miles (29 kilometers) across.

Quick Practice

Directions: Draw a line between the subject and the predicate.

People take helicopter rides into the canyon.

NAME: ____________________ **DATE:** ______________

Directions: Check for spelling errors in the paragraph. Use the symbol to correct them. **Hint:** There are four spelling mistakes.

The Grand Canyon, located in northurn Arizona, is won of the Seven Wonders of the World. It is an extremely large canyon maid of red rock. The Colorado River runs threw the bottom of the canyon. This is how the canyon was created; the Colorado River has run through the canyon for about two billion years. Nearly five million people visit the Grand Canyon each year.

Quick Practice

Directions: Write the plural form of each noun.

1. pyramid ____________________
2. country ____________________
3. body ____________________

NAME: ______________________ **DATE:** ________________

Directions: Reread the paragraph. Think about how you can improve it based on what you have practiced throughout the week. Add your notes in the margins. Then, rewrite the new and improved paragraph on the lines below.

The Grand Canyon is locates in Arizona. It's 277 miles (446 kilometers) long. It is one of the large canyons in the world. The Colorado River runs threw the Grand Canyon. Native Americans have lived around the Grand Canyon for thousands of years. People enjoys visiting this beautiful place. Visitors often hike the canyon or go rafting on the river.

This week I learned:

- how to identify incomplete sentences
- how to identify correct adjectives
- how to edit spelling errors

© Shell Education

NAME: ______________________________ **DATE:** ____________________

Directions: Place check marks in the pyramids with complete sentences.

- The pyramids of Egypt.
- They vary in size.
- It took a long time to build each pyramid.
- Built by humans.
- The pyramids are fascinating.
- The base of a pyramid is square.

NAME: ______________________ **DATE:** ________________

Directions: Think about Egyptian pyramids. Draft an informative/explanatory paragraph about Egyptian pyramids. Include facts about what they look like and how they are used.

Remember!

A strong informative/explanatory paragraph should include:

- a topic sentence
- details to support the main idea
- a concluding sentence

Printing Practice

Directions: Use your best printing to write the proper noun *Egypt* two times.

 © Shell Education

NAME: ____________________ **DATE:** ________________

Directions: Choose the correct adjective from the Word Bank to complete each sentence.

Word Bank

smaller largest tallest longer most

1. The ancient Egyptian pyramids are some of the ________________ impressive structures ever built by humans.
2. The ________________ pyramid is the Pyramid of Khufu, also known as the Great Pyramid of Giza.
3. For years, the Pyramid of Khufu was considered the ________________ man-made structure, reaching over 480 feet (146 meters) tall.
4. It took much ________________ to build then than it would today.
5. The ________________ rooms within the pyramids were usually temples.

Time to Improve!

Go back to the draft you wrote on page 100. Did you use any superlative or comparative adjectives? If you did, make sure you used them correctly.

NAME: ______________________________ **DATE:** ________________

Directions: Use the ≡, the ∧, and the ℓ symbols to edit the paragraph.
Hint: There are six mistakes.

Their are many unique facts about the pyramids. The Great Pyramid of giza points to the north. The pyramids of egypt were all built to the west of the nile River. The base of the pyramid was always a perfect square The pyramids were built mostly of limestone. They're were traps and curses put on the pyramids to try to keep the robbers out. Its unbelievable how advanced the culture was thousands of years ago.

Time to Improve!

Go back to the draft you wrote on page 100. Reread your writing to make sure that you spelled and capitalized the words correctly.

 © Shell Education

NAME: ______________________ **DATE:** ________________

Directions: Think about Egyptian pyramids. Write an informative/explanatory paragraph about Egyptian pyramids. Include facts about what they look like and how they are used.

© Shell Education

NAME: ______________________________ **DATE:** ____________________

Directions: Read the statements about Thomas Edison. Place a check mark next to each sentence that you would want to include in a narrative paragraph about meeting him.

_____ Thomas Edison was born in Milan, Ohio, but later moved to Michigan.

_____ Thomas Edison was homeschooled by his mother.

_____ Edison was smart and friendly.

_____ Edison knew he would be an inventor.

_____ He was in his early thirties when he invented a lightbulb that could be made and used for the home.

_____ He also invented safety fuses and on-and-off switches for light sockets.

_____ Edison was fun to be around.

_____ He continued working and inventing until his death in 1931.

 © Shell Education

NAME: ______________________ **DATE:** ________________

Directions: Read the paragraph. Draft notes in the margins about which parts of the paragraph help you know that it is a narrative.

One day, I was walking through the park. Out of nowhere, I bumped into a man named Thomas Edison. He was very nice and polite even though I ran into him. He was in his early thirties and explained to me that he was an inventor. I didn't recognize him at first, but when I asked him about the inventions he created, I realized that I should have known who he was. He invented the lightbulb for the home! He also invented safety fuses and on-and-off switches for light sockets. Imagine that! I use all of the items every day, and I didn't even recognize the man who made them possible. Embarrassed, I politely thanked him for talking with me and then walked away. I will now think of this day every time I turn on the lights in my home.

Cursive Practice *abc*

Directions: Write the words *inventor* and *lightbulb* in cursive.

____

____

NAME: ______________________ DATE: ______________

Directions: Revise the simple sentences to make compound sentences.

1. Thomas Edison may be the greatest inventor in history. He has over 1,000 patents.

 ____

 ____

2. Thomas Edison built a research laboratory. The lab was built for the purpose of inventing.

 ____

 ____

3. Thomas Edison was born in Milan, Ohio. He later moved to Michigan.

 ____

 ____

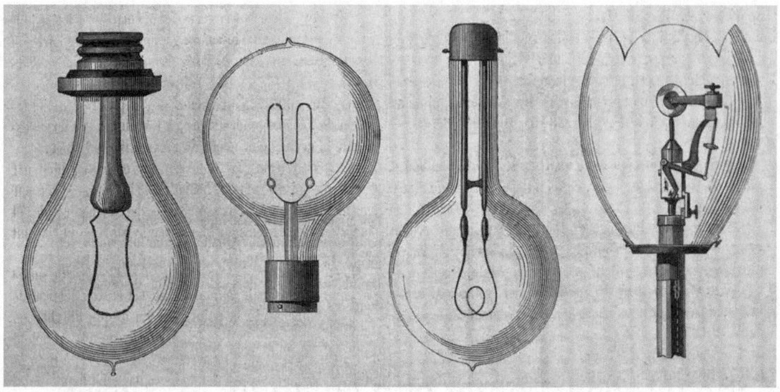

Boost Your Learning!

To vary your writing, try to include compound sentences.

Simple Sentences: Thomas Edison was an entrepreneur. He started many companies.

Compound Sentence: Thomas Edison was an entrepreneur, and he started many companies.

NAME: ____________________ **DATE:** ____________________

Directions: Use the ∧ symbol to add commas in the addresses.

Boost Your Learning!

When writing an address, a comma separates the city from the state.

Example: 468 Sunny Dr.
Sacramento, CA 95828

NAME: ______________________ **DATE:** ________________

Directions: Reread the paragraph. In the margins, add at least two lines of dialogue. Then, draw arrows to where the dialogue should be placed in the paragraph.

One day, I was walking through the park. Out of nowhere, I bumped into a man named Thomas Edison. He was very nice and polite even though I ran into him. He was in his early thirties and explained to me that he was an inventor. I didn't recognize him at first, but when I asked him about the inventions he created, I realized that I should have known who he was. He invented the lightbulb for the home! He also invented safety fuses and on-and-off switches for light sockets. Imagine that! I use all of the items every day, and I didn't even recognize the man who made them possible. Embarrassed, I politely thanked him for talking with me and then walked away. I will now think of this day every time I turn on the lights in my home.

This week I learned:

- how to write compound sentences
- how to add commas to addresses

 © Shell Education

NAME: ______________________ **DATE:** ________________

Directions: Read the facts about Benjamin Franklin. Then, use the chart below to plan what you would like to include in a narrative paragraph about meeting him.

- Benjamin Franklin was a great American.
- He was able to start several companies and create four different inventions.
- Franklin did not patent any inventions because he preferred people use them for their own convenience.
- His inventions include electricity, the Franklin stove, bifocal lenses, and the lightning rod.
- Franklin was a very influential man in his time.

My Day with Benjamin Franklin
Where we met:
What he was like:
What we did:

NAME: ____________________ **DATE:** ____________________

Directions: Draft a narrative paragraph about meeting Benjamin Franklin. Include details about what happened when you met him. Use your notes from page 109 to help you draft your paragraph.

Remember!

A strong narrative paragraph:

- includes an introductory and a concluding sentence
- uses sensory details to describe the experience
- makes it sound like a story

Cursive Practice

Directions: Use cursive to complete the sentence.

I would like to invent ____________________.

 © Shell Education

NAME: ______________________ **DATE:** ________________

Directions: Read each sentence. Label each sentence *simple* if the sentence is simple and *compound* if the sentence is compound.

1. Benjamin Franklin was a great American.

   ____

2. He was able to start several companies and create four different inventions.

   ____

3. Franklin did not patent any inventions because he preferred that people use them for their own convenience.

   ____

4. His inventions include electricity, the Franklin stove, bifocal lenses, and the lightning rod.

   ____

5. Franklin was a very influential man in his time.

   ____

Time to Improve!

Go back to the draft you wrote on page 110. Look for simple sentences. Try revising some of them to make them compound sentences.

NAME: ______________________ **DATE:** ____________________

Directions: Use the ∧ symbol to add commas to the following sentences.

1. Benjamin Franklin was born in Boston Massachusetts.

2. He spent some time working in London England.

3. Benjamin Franklin was the chief delegate to the congress in Albany New York.

4. Franklin died in Philadelphia Pennsylvania.

Quick Practice

Directions: Think of three adjectives that describe Benjamin Franklin.

1. ______________________

2. ______________________

3. ______________________

Time to Improve!

Go back to the draft you wrote on page 110. Check to make sure that you have correctly used commas.

 © Shell Education

NAME: ______________________ **DATE:** ________________

Directions: Write a narrative paragraph about meeting Benjamin Franklin. Include details about what happened when you met him.

NAME: ______________________ **DATE:** ______________

Directions: Place check marks in the circles with sentences that could be included in an informative/explanatory paragraph.

Octopuses

- Octopuses have eight arms.
- An octopus's tentacles allow it to grab objects.
- Octopuses are the coolest sea animals.
- I would like to have an octopus as a pet.
- Octopuses come in all sorts of colors.
- An octopus has no bones in its body.

 © Shell Education

NAME: ______________________ **DATE:** ________________

Directions: Read the paragraph. Write notes in the margins explaining why the paragraph is an informative/explanatory paragraph.

Octopuses have some interesting ways of defending themselves. They can blend into their surroundings, allowing them to hide easily from predators. They can also protect themselves by squirting an inky substance at predators, blinding them temporarily. The ink has a way of lessening a predator's sense of smell as well. This makes it hard for predators to see and smell the octopuses, giving them time to get away safely.

Cursive Practice *abc*

Directions: Write two adjectives that describe an octopus in cursive.

______________________ ______________________

______________________ ______________________

NAME: ______________________ **DATE:** ________________

Directions: Underline the coordinating conjunction in each sentence.

1. Octopuses can live in warm and cold water, and they can weigh up to 55 pounds (25 kilograms).

2. The blue-ringed octopus is beautiful and small, but it's one of the most poisonous animals on Earth.

3. A squid has no skeletal structure, nor does the octopus.

4. The areas around the eyes, arms, and suckers may get dark, so an octopus appears more threatening.

5. Octopuses can reach speeds of 25 mph (40 kph), but they cannot maintain this speed for too long.

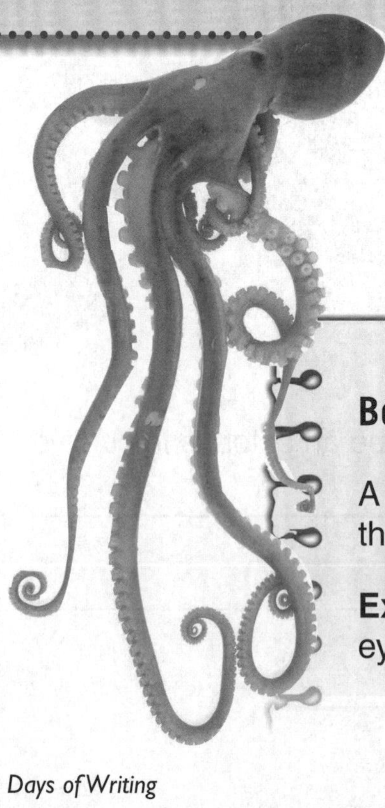

Boost Your Learning!

A **coordinating conjunction** is a word that connects parts of a sentence.

Example: Octopuses have excellent eyesight, **but** they are deaf.

NAME: ______________________ DATE: ________________

Directions: Use the ℘ symbol to correct misspelled words in the paragraph.

Octopuses have sum interesting weighs of defending themselves. They can blend into their surroundings, allowing them to hyde easily from predators. They can also protect themselves by squirting an inky substance at predators, blinding them temporarily. The ink has a way of lessening a predator's cents of smell as well. This makes it hard for predators to sea and smell the octopuses, giving them time to get away safely.

Remember!

Some words sound the same, but they have different meanings and spellings. Be sure to use the correct spellings of these words in your writing. If you come across a word that might be spelled incorrectly, circle it and write *sp* above the circle. If you know how to spell the word correctly, cross out the word in the sentence and write the word correctly above it.

© Shell Education

NAME: ______________________ **DATE:** ________________

Directions: Reread the paragraph about the octopus. Then, add two new details to the paragraph and rewrite a final version below. Use the sentences on page 116 to help you.

Octopuses have some interesting ways of defending themselves. They can blend into their surroundings, allowing them to hide easily from predators. They can also protect themselves by squirting an inky substance at predators, blinding them temporarily. The ink has a way of lessening a predator's sense of smell as well. This makes it hard for predators to see and smell the octopuses, giving them time to get away safely.

____

____

____

____

____

____

____

____

This week I learned:

- how to identity coordinating conjunctions
- how to identify multiple meaning words

 © Shell Education

NAME: ______________________ **DATE:** ________________

Directions: Label the picture of the shark. Use the terms in the Word Bank to help you.

Word Bank

skinny gills	beady eye	rough skin
small fin	sharp teeth	pointy snout

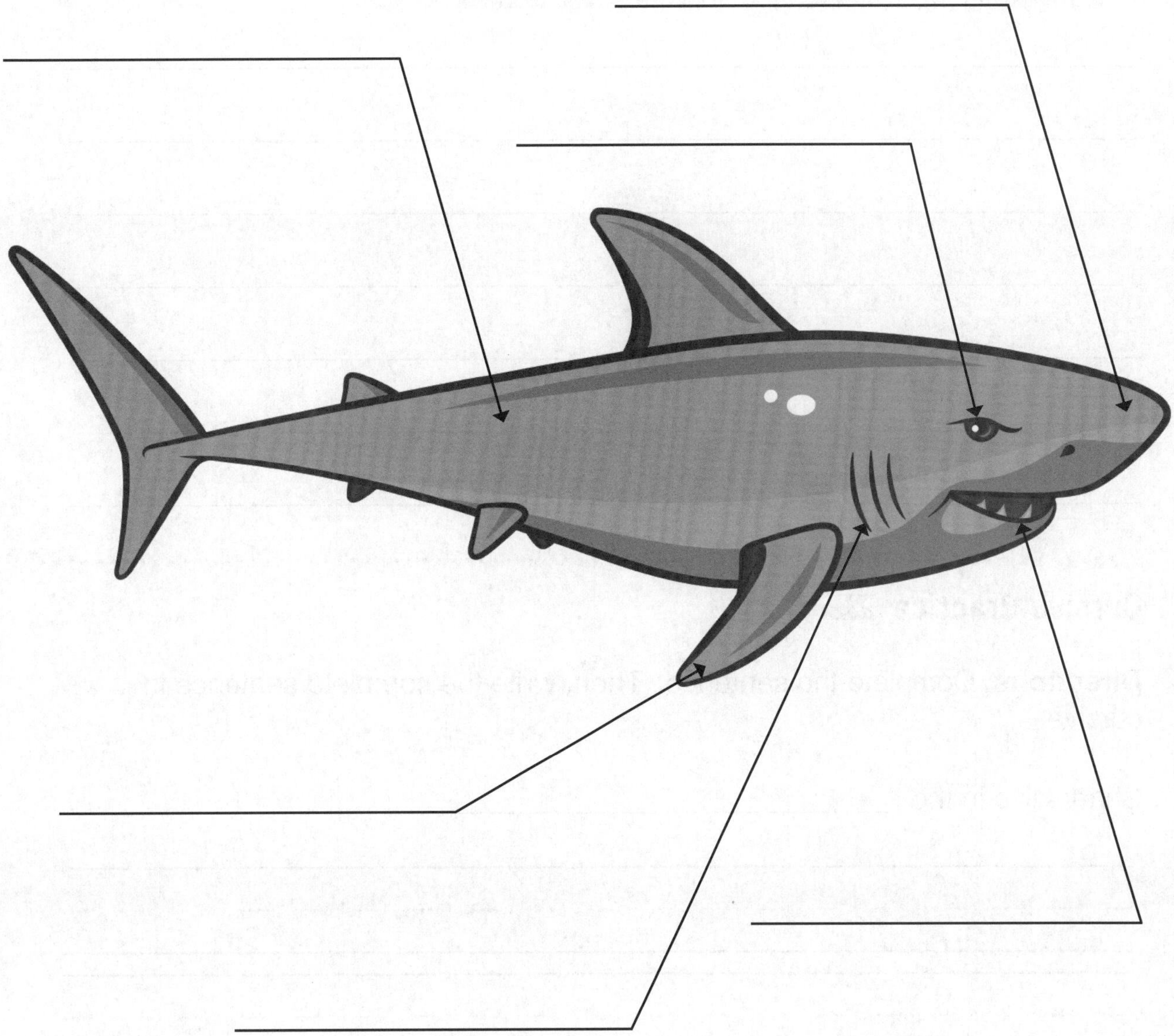

NAME: ______________________ **DATE:** ______________

Directions: Think about sharks. Draft an informative/explanatory paragraph about sharks. Include facts about what they eat and what they look like. Use your notes on page 119 and the facts below to help you draft your paragraph.

Fact Bank

- They swim in large, deep oceans.
- Sharks are able to smell from very far away.
- They breathe through gills.
- A shark's skin is made of rough scales.

____

____

____

____

____

____

____

Cursive Practice *abc*

Directions: Complete the sentence. Then, write the complete sentence in cursive.

Sharks live in the ______________________________.

____

____

NAME: ______________________ **DATE:** ________________

Directions: Insert a coordinating conjunction to complete each sentence.

1. Sharks have been around for nearly 400 million years ____________ are on top of the ocean's natural food chain.

2. They're such good survivors, ____________ they've had little reason to evolve over the last 150 million years.

3. Many people fear sharks, ____________ they are quite harmless to humans most of the time.

Remember!

A coordinating conjunction is a word that connects parts of a sentence. Coordinating conjunctions include: *for*, *and*, *nor*, *but*, *or*, *yet*, and *so*.

Time to Improve!

Go back to the draft you wrote on page 120. Did you include coordinating conjunctions? If you did not, see if you can add some in.

NAME: ____________________ **DATE:** ____________

Editing : Sharks

Directions: Use the ℘ symbol to correct spelling errors in the sentences.

1. Sharks have an incredible sense of smell, makeing them very successful predators.

2. Sharks are fascinating for both adults and childs.

3. They have the most powerfull jaws on the planet.

4. Each tipe of shark has a different-shape tooth.

5. Sharks never run out of teeth because they have rows of backup tooths.

Remember!

When you come across a word that might be spelled incorrectly, circle it and write *sp* above the circle. If you know how to spell the word correctly, cross out the word in the sentence and write the word correctly above it.

Time to Improve!

Go back to the draft you wrote on page 120. Reread the paragraph to make sure you spelled everything correctly.

© Shell Education

NAME: ______________________ **DATE:** ______________

Directions: Think about sharks. Write an informative/explanatory paragraph about sharks. Include facts about what they eat and what they look like.

NAME: ______________________________ **DATE:** ____________________

Directions: Place stars in the planets that have sentences you think belong in an informative/explanatory paragraph about planets.

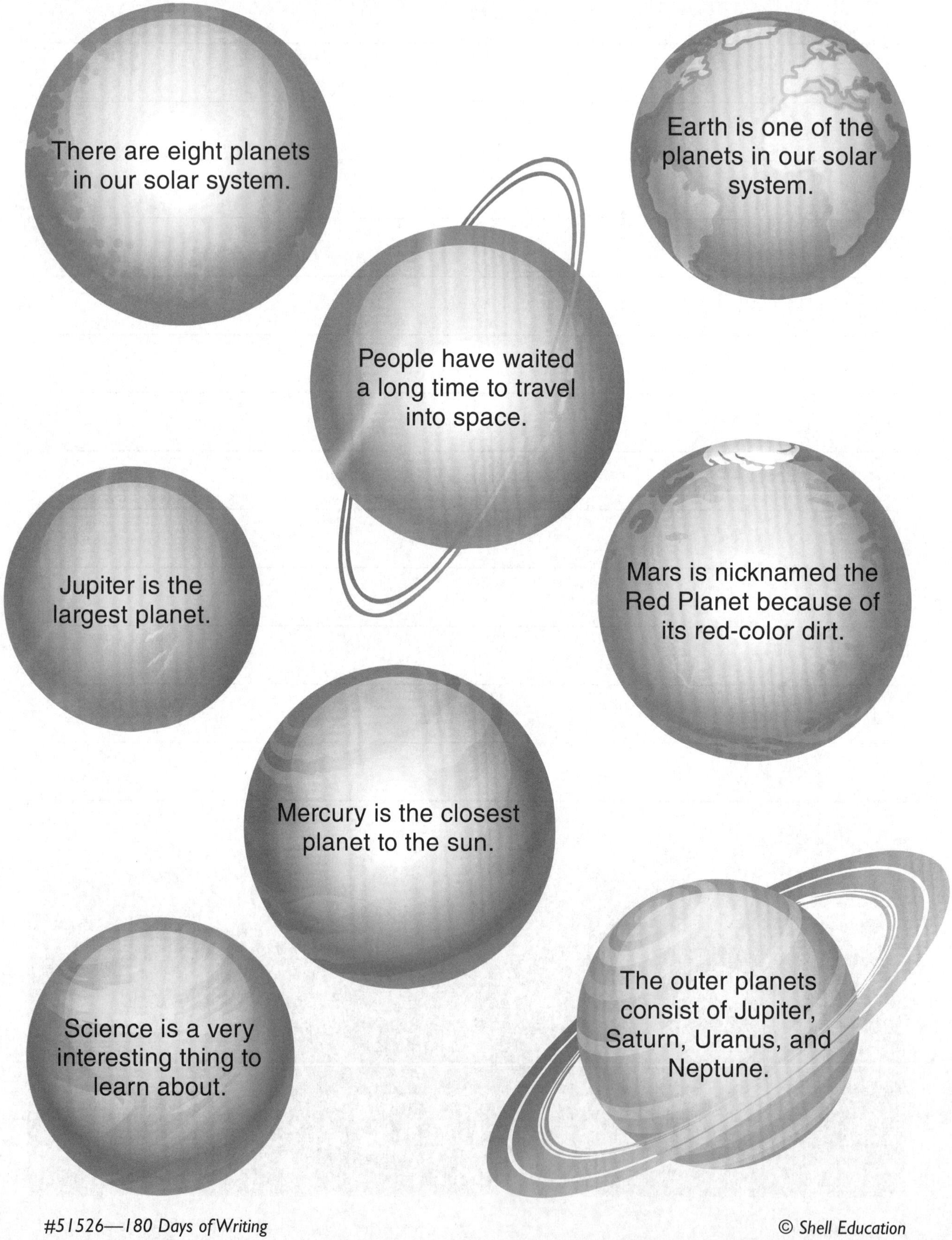

 © Shell Education

NAME: ______________________ **DATE:** ________________

Directions: Read the paragraph. Cross out sentences that do not stay on topic.

There are eight planets in our solar system, including our planet, Earth. I like rockets. Jupiter is the largest planet. Mars is nicknamed the Red Planet because of its red-color dirt. People enjoy watching space movies. Mercury and Venus are the closest planets to the sun. The outer planets consist of Jupiter, Saturn, Uranus, and Neptune. Would you travel to space?

Cursive Practice *abc*

Directions: Pick two planets and write their names in cursive.

NAME: ______________________ **DATE:** ________________

Directions: Circle the correct adjective to make each sentence complete.

1. Earth has (fewer **or** fewest) moons than Jupiter.
2. Venus is the (brighter **or** brightest) planet in our solar system.
3. Earth has (more **or** most) water than land.
4. Mars has the (larger **or** largest) volcano in the solar system.
5. The red spot of Jupiter is the (bigger **or** biggest), most violent storm in the universe.
6. Saturn is the (lighter **or** lightest) planet in our solar system.

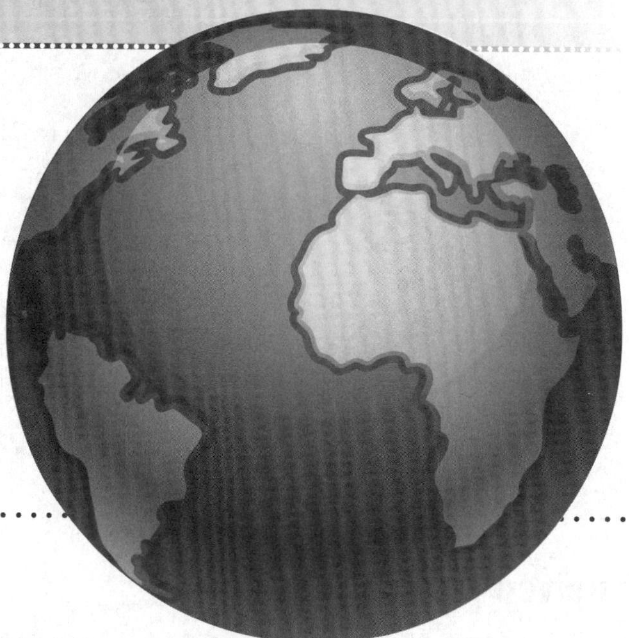

Quick Practice

Directions: Place commas where necessary.

1. The inner planets are Mercury Venus Earth and Mars.
2. The solar system also contains comets dust moons and some dwarf planets.

© Shell Education

NAME: ______________________ **DATE:** ________________

Directions: Use the ≡ and / symbols to correct the capitalization errors in the paragraph.

There are eight Planets in our solar system. pluto was the former ninth planet but has since been named a dwarf planet. sometime, venus can be seen with the human eye because it's the brightest planet. jupiter is so large that all the other planets could fit inside it! Both Saturn and uranus have rings made of Rock and ice. Neptune, like jupiter, has a dark spot caused by a storm. Planets are quite interesting, and scientists are always learning new facts about them.

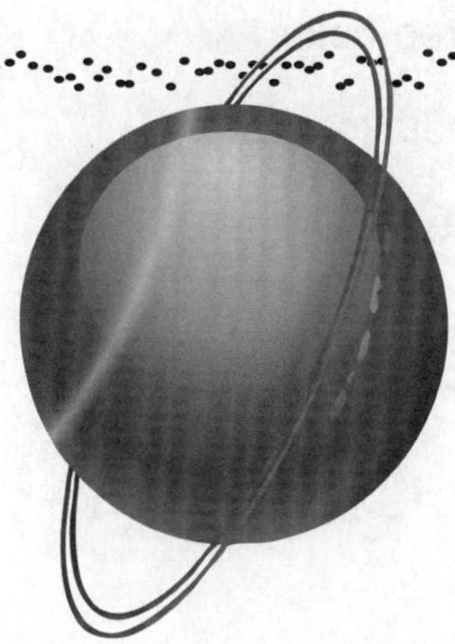

Remember!

Proper nouns and the first words in sentences must start with capital letters. Common nouns are not capitalized.

NAME: ______________________ **DATE:** ______________

Publishing
Planets

Directions: Read the paragraph. Use the margins to add the two details in the Detail Bank to the paragraph.

Detail Bank

- An interesting fact about Saturn is its many moons; it has has about 53 known moons.
- Venus's yellow clouds reflect the sun's light brightly.

There are eight planets in our solar system, including our planet, Earth. Jupiter is the largest planet. Mars is nicknamed the Red Planet because of its red-color dirt. Mercury and Venus are the closest planets to the sun. The outer planets consist of Jupiter, Saturn, Uranus, and Neptune.

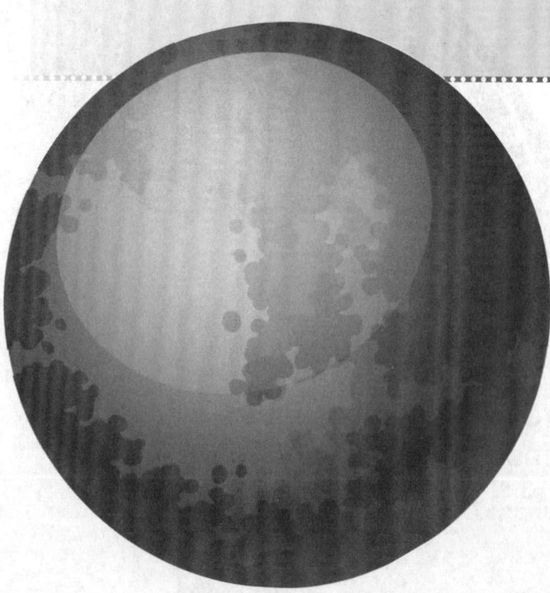

This week I learned:

- how to identify proper nouns
- how to use comparative and superlative adjectives
- how to edit for correct capitalization

 © Shell Education

NAME: ______________________ **DATE:** ________________

Directions: Draw pictures of the sun and the moon. Write one thing that is similar between them and one thing that is different.

Sun	Moon

Similarity

____

____

Difference

____

____

NAME: ______________________ **DATE:** ______________

Directions: Think about the sun and the moon. Draft an informative/explanatory paragraph about the most interesting facts about them. Discuss their similarities and differences, too. Use your notes from page 129 to help you.

Remember!

A strong informative/explanatory paragraph should include:

- a topic sentence
- details to support the main idea
- a concluding sentence

Cursive Practice *abc*

Directions: Use cursive to write the words *sun* and *moon*.

  © Shell Education

NAME: ______________________ **DATE:** ______________

Directions: Write the correct form of the comparative or superlative adjectives in the blanks.

1. Our moon is the fifth ______________________ (large) moon in the solar system.

2. Mons Huygens is the ______________________ (tall) mountain on the moon.

3. The effect of gravity is much ______________________ (strong) on Earth than on the moon.

4. Earth is much ______________________ (close) to the sun than to any other star.

5. The sun is over one million times ______________________ (big) than Earth.

Quick Practice

Directions: Underline the possessive nouns in the sentences

1. The sun's surface is scorching hot.

2. Earth's tides are largely caused by the gravitational pull of the moon.

3. The moon's surface is covered with craters.

Time to Improve!

Go back to the draft you wrote on page 130. Did you use any comparative or superlative adjectives in your writing? If you did, make sure you used them correctly.

© Shell Education

NAME: ______________________________ **DATE:** ____________________

Editing
Sun and Moon

Directions: Use the ≡ and / symbols to correct the capitalization errors in the sentences.

1. the first Person to set foot on the Moon was neil armstrong.

2. a lunar eclipse occurs when earth is between the Sun and the Moon.

3. the Moon orbits earth every 27.3 days.

4. many civilizations have worshipped the Sun because of its great importance.

5. a solar eclipse Occurs when the Moon is between Earth and the sun.

Boost Your Learning!

The words *moon* and *sun* should not be capitalized unless they come at the beginning of a sentence.

Time to Improve!

Go back to the draft you wrote on page 130. Check to make sure that all of your words are capitalized and lowercased correctly.

 © Shell Education

NAME: ______________________ **DATE:** ________________

Directions: Think about the sun and the moon. Write an informative/explanatory paragraph about the most interesting facts about them. Discuss their similarities and differences, too.

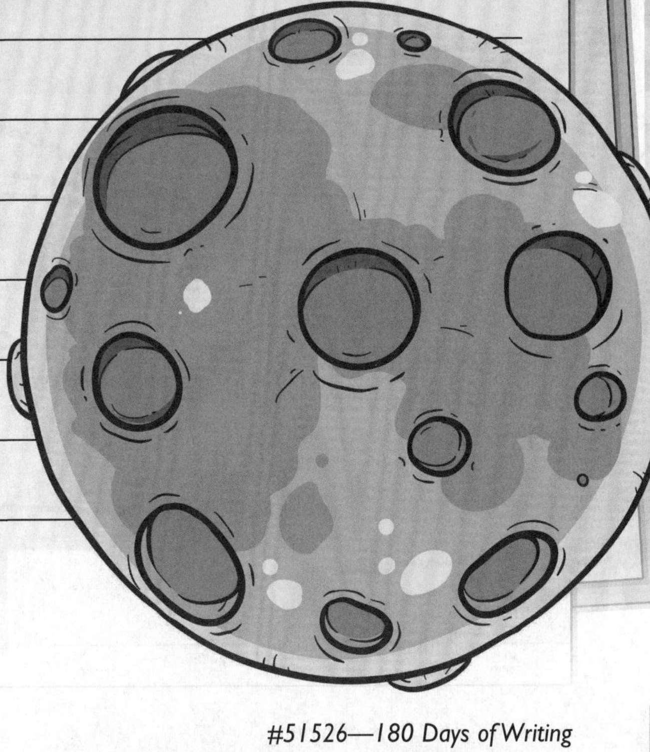

NAME: ______________________ **DATE:** ________________

Directions: Place check marks in the books with questions you would ask author Eric Carle about his career.

Do you like chocolate ice cream?

Which book that you have written is the most meaningful to you?

Do you like to swim, hike, or jog?

What other jobs have you had?

What are the steps you take when writing a book?

How many family members do you have?

When did you start drawing?

What is the title of the first book you wrote?

© Shell Education

NAME: ______________________ **DATE:** ________________

Directions: Read the dialogue. Then, answer the question.

"I want to be an author like you when I grow up," said Molly.

"You can be anything you want, as long as you work hard," Eric Carle stated.

"I am willing to work extra hard. I promise," Molly said with a smile. "One day, you'll be reading a book by the famous Molly," she announced.

1. How does the dialogue help the reader understand the text?

____

____

____

____

Cursive Practice *abc*

Directions: Use cursive to complete the sentence.

My favorite book is . . .

____

____

NAME: ______________________ **DATE:** ________________

Revising
Eric Carle

Directions: Read the paragraph. Circle the verbs that are not in the present tense. Then, write the verbs correctly below.

Eric Carle used the technique of collage when he created his beautiful pictures. He painted over colored tissue paper and created texture by using different objects such as paintbrushes, his fingers, sponges, or even stamps. Then, he cuts out different shapes to made his scenes and characters.

1. ______________________
2. ______________________
3. ______________________
4. ______________________
5. ______________________

Quick Practice

Directions: Circle the words that have more than one meaning.

pencil watch tree bat trunk

 © Shell Education

NAME: ______________________ **DATE:** ______________

Directions: Use the ∨ symbol to add quotation marks to the dialogue.

I want to be an author when I grow up, said Molly.

You can be anything you want, as long as you work hard, Eric Carle stated.

I am willing to work extra hard. I promise, Molly said with a smile. One day, you'll be reading a book by the famous Molly, she announced.

NAME: ______________________ **DATE:** ______________

Directions: Revisit the dialogue. Think about what might come next in the dialogue between Molly and Eric Carle. Then, add at least two more lines of dialogue.

"I want to be an author like you when I grow up," said Molly.

"You can be anything you want, as long as you work hard," Eric Carle stated.

"I am willing to work extra hard. I promise," Molly said with a smile. "One day, you'll be reading a book by the famous Molly," she announced.

____

____

____

____

____

____

____

This week I learned:

- how to use consistent verb tense
- how to use correct punctuation in dialogue

 © Shell Education

NAME: ______________________ **DATE:** ________________

Directions: Imagine you get to interview J.K. Rowling, author of the Harry Potter series. Create a question for each word below. The first one is done for you.

1. **sleep:** Do any of your ideas come to you while you are sleeping?
2. **think:** ______________________
3. **edit:** ______________________
4. **play:** ______________________
5. **spell:** ______________________
6. **erase:** ______________________
7. **rewrite:** ______________________
8. **give up:** ______________________

NAME: ______________________ **DATE:** ________________

Directions: Imagine you are interviewing J.K. Rowling. What would you ask her? What would you discuss? Draft a made-up dialogue between the two of you. Include at least three questions with corresponding answers. Use your questions from page 139 to help draft your narrative paragraph.

Remember!

A strong narrative paragraph:

- includes an introductory and a concluding sentence
- uses sensory details to describe the experience
- makes it sound like a story

Cursive Practice

Directions: Use cursive to write the words *author* and *series*.

© Shell Education

NAME: ______________________ **DATE:** ________________

Directions: Read the paragraph. Circle the verbs that are not in past tense. Then, answer the question.

J.K. Rowling is born in England on July 31, 1965. As a child, she enjoys playing make-believe games with her younger sister, Diane. She goes to school and studied hard. She later studied French at the University of Exeter. Rowling said she is on a train when she imagined the first *Harry Potter* book. *Harry Potter* became a phenomenon, and Rowling goes on to write six more *Harry Potter* books.

1. Why is it important for verbs to stay in the same tense?

____

____

____

____

Time to Improve!

Go back to the draft you wrote on page 140. Check to make sure that all of your verbs are in the same tense. If they are not, revise them.

NAME: ______________________ **DATE:** ______________

Editing

J.K. Rowling

Directions: Use the ∨ symbol to add quotation marks to the sentences.

1. I want to meet J.K. Rowling! exclaimed Samantha.

2. Brian whispered, I wish I were a famous author.

3. Writing takes a lot of concentration, said Mrs. Temple.

4. I still need to edit and revise my story, Mary said. I cannot publish it quite yet.

5. It's hard to believe J.K. Rowling went from being unemployed to being a millionaire in just five years, Mom stated.

Quick Practice

Directions: Use context clues to figure out the meaning of the underlined word. Then, write it on the line.

The author became frazzled after her publisher gave her a long list of things to change.

____

Time to Improve!

Go back to the draft you wrote on page 140. Did you add dialogue to your narrative? If you did not, try to add some. Make sure that you use commas and quotation marks correctly.

 © Shell Education

NAME: ______________________________ **DATE:** ____________________

Directions: Imagine you are interviewing J.K. Rowling. What would you ask her? What would you discuss? Write a made-up dialogue between the two of you. Include at least three questions with corresponding answers.

© Shell Education

NAME: ______________________ **DATE:** ______________

Directions: Use the words in the Word Bank to label the life cycle of a butterfly. Then, write a sentence showing what you know about the life cycle.

Word Bank

pupa larvae egg adult

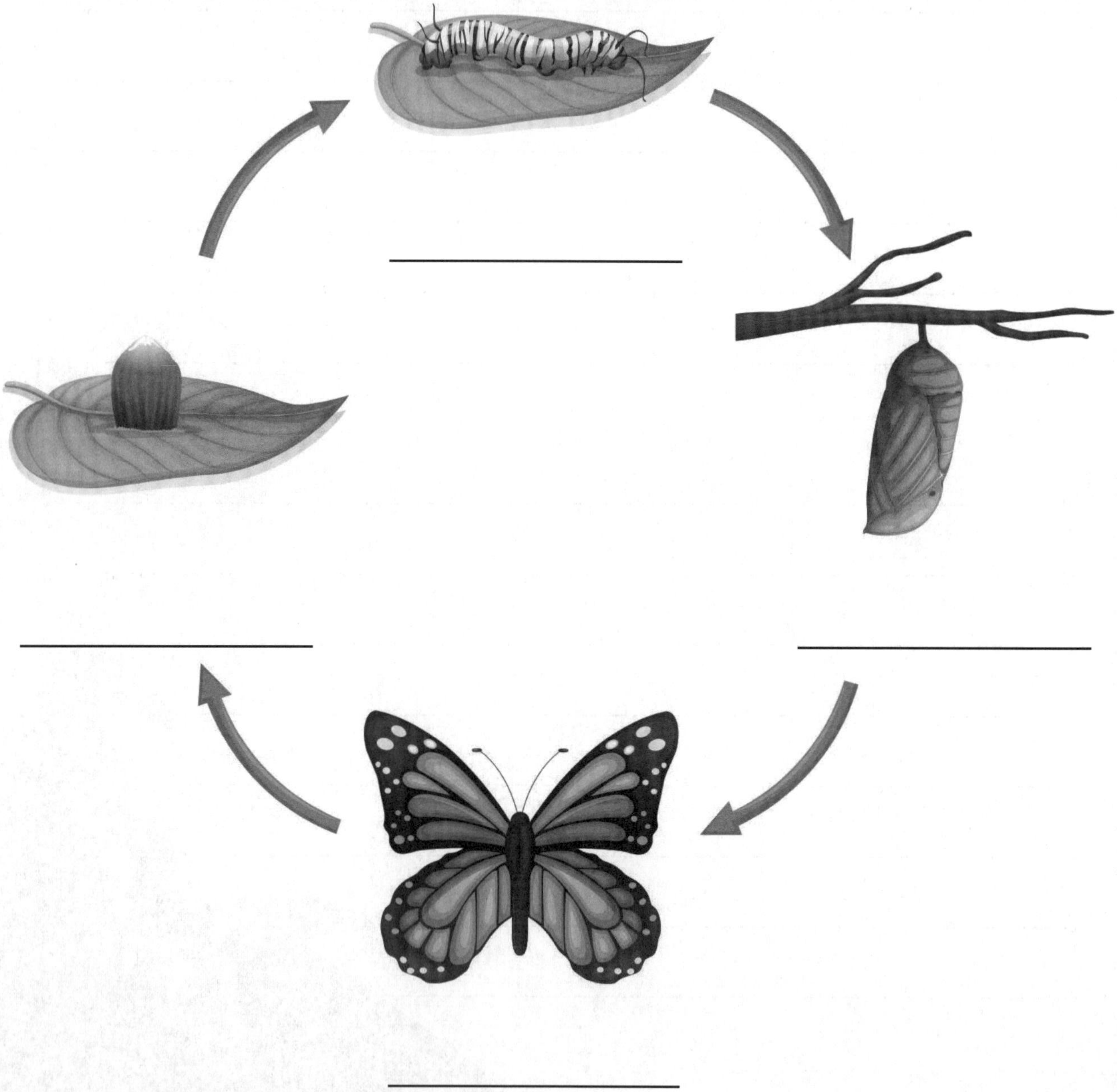

____

____

NAME: ______________________ **DATE:** ________________

Directions: Read the paragraph. Underline the opinion sentences. Then, answer the questions.

Insects have six legs. Butterflies are peaceful to watch. There are about 28,000 species of butterflies in the world. The four stages of metamorphosis are interesting and complex. Butterflies have three body parts.

1. How can the author improve the opinion paragraph?

2. Do you agree with the author's opinion? Why or why not?

Remember!

An opinion states a feeling or a thought.

Cursive Practice

Directions: Use cursive to write the words *insect* and *eggs*.

NAME: ______________________ **DATE:** ______________

Directions: Read the original sentence. Write a list of adjectives that would make the sentence more interesting. Then, use some of the adjectives to write a new and improved opinion sentence.

Original Sentence

Butterflies are insects.

Adjectives about Butterflies

- ✓ ______________________
- ✓ ______________________
- ✓ ______________________
- ✓ ______________________
- ✓ ______________________
- ✓ ______________________

My New and Improved Opinion Sentence

____

____

____

 © Shell Education

NAME: ______________________ **DATE:** ________________

Directions: Use the ∧ symbol to add adverbs from the Word Bank to the sentences.

Word Bank

carefully slowly patiently brightly

1. The colored wings of butterflies are fascinating.

2. The adult butterfly will emerge from the pupa.

3. Adult butterflies must wait for their wings to dry before their first flight.

4. Fully grown caterpillars must attach themselves to twigs or branches before shedding their skin.

Boost Your Learning!

Adverbs tell about verbs.

Example: The butterfly **quietly** rests on the tree branch.

NAME: ______________________ **DATE:** ______________

Directions: Read the paragraph. Then, answer the questions.

Butterflies are the most amazing insects in the world. They have six legs. Butterflies are peaceful to watch. There are about 15,000 to 20,000 species of butterflies in the world. The four stages of metamorphosis are interesting and complex. Butterflies have three body parts.

1. Is this a strong opinion paragraph? Why or why not?

____

____

____

2. What advice can you give the author to improve this paragraph?

____

____

____

This week I learned:

- how to identify statements and opinions
- how to use adjectives to make my writing more interesting
- how to add adverbs to sentences

© Shell Education

NAME: ______________________ **DATE:** ______________

Directions: Read the facts about bees. Do you find bees interesting? Write at least two notes to support why bees are interesting and why they might not be interesting.

- Bees are insects.
- If a worker bee uses her stinger, she will die.
- Bees have two stomachs.
- Bees have two pairs of wings.
- Worker bees are all female.
- Only the queen in the hive lays eggs.

Why Bees Are Interesting	**Why Bees Are Not Interesting**

Drafting: Bees

NAME: ____________________ **DATE:** ____________________

Directions: Do you think bees are interesting? Draft a paragraph expressing your opinion. Give at least three reasons to support your opinion. Use your notes from page 149 to help you draft your opinion paragraph.

Remember!

A strong opinion paragraph includes:

- an introductory sentence
- details that support your opinion
- a concluding sentence

Cursive Practice

Directions: Use cursive to complete the sentence.

Bees are . . .

© Shell Education

NAME: ______________________ **DATE:** ______________

Directions: Read the factual statements. Then, turn each one into an opinion statement.

Example

Statement: Male bees are called drones.

Opinion: It's interesting how male bees are called *drones*.

1. A queen bee can lay up to 1,500 eggs a day.

____

____

2. There is only one queen bee in an entire colony.

____

____

Quick Practice

Directions: Write one word for each part of speech.

1. noun: ______________________
2. verb: ______________________
3. adjective: ______________________
4. adverb: ______________________

Time to Improve!

Go back to the draft you wrote on page 150. Check to make sure you included your opinion in it. If some of the sentences don't support the opinion, revise them.

NAME: ______________________ **DATE:** ______________

Directions: Use the ∧ symbol to add at least three adverbs to the paragraph.

Worker bees have the toughest job of all bees. Their list of duties includes taking care of the babies, feeding the queen bee, cleaning the hive, packing pollen and nectar into cells, building and repairing honeycombs, and guarding the hive. It's no wonder that they only live three to six weeks long. Even though their lives are short, they are valuable.

Time to Improve!

Go back to the draft you wrote on page 150. Did you include adverbs in your writing? If you did not, try to add some.

 © Shell Education

NAME: ______________________ DATE: ________________

Directions: Do you think bees are interesting? Write a paragraph expressing your opinion. Give at least three reasons to support your opinion.

NAME: ______________________ DATE: ________________

Directions: Look at the cookies. Write a sentence describing each one.

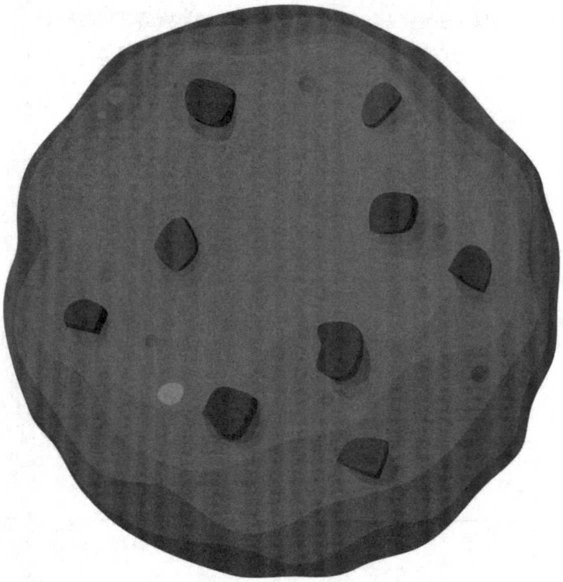

____

____

____

____

____

____

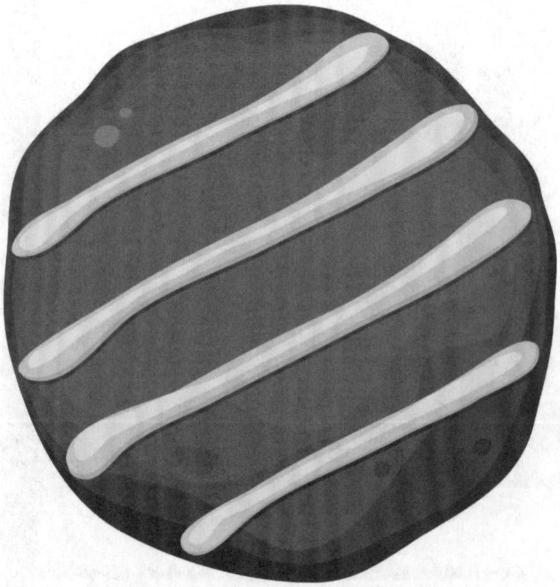

____

____

____

 © Shell Education

NAME: ______________________ **DATE:** ________________

Directions: Read the opinion paragraph. Each sentence should contain a noun. Underline the nouns, and then place each noun in the appropriate column below.

Cookies are the best dessert. There are so many different types to choose from. They go well with a glass of milk. Dunking them is so much fun! They are versatile and come in many sizes. The different ingredients are endless; the best are chocolate chips and sprinkles. There's a flavor and size for everyone.

Singular	Plural

Cursive Practice

Directions: Complete the sentence. Then, rewrite the sentence in cursive.

I don't care for ______________________ cookies.

NAME: ______________________ **DATE:** ________________

Revising
Cookies

Directions: Read the sentences. Then, write pronouns for the underlined words.

1. Baking cookies is so much fun! Baking cookies is easy to do, too!

   ____

2. Sally loves putting chocolate chips in the mixture. Sally's mom carefully folds them into the batter.

   ____

3. The cookies bake for 15 minutes, and then they need time to cool. Once cooled, Mom and I enjoy the cookies.

   ____

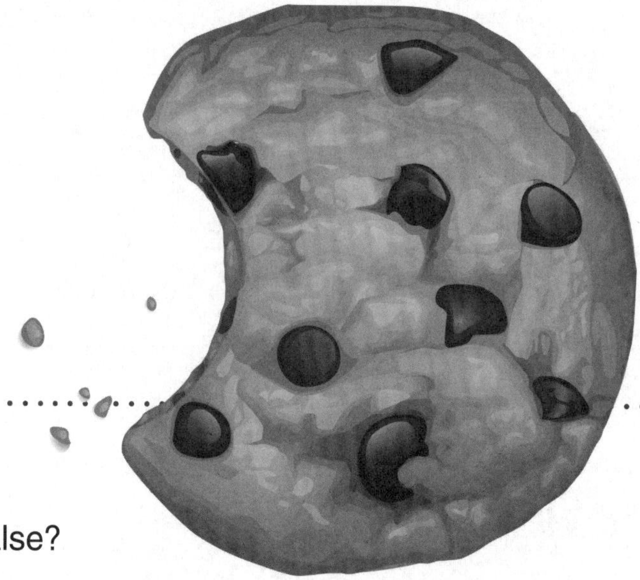

Quick Practice

Directions: True or False?

1. A comma is used to separate the city from the state.

   ____

2. Commas are used to separate the month from the date.

   ____

 © Shell Education

NAME: ______________________ **DATE:** ________________

Directions: Use the ≡ symbol to capitalize the appropriate words in the book titles.

1. *cookies are yummy* by Sara Smith

2. *baking bliss* by Henry Case

3. *the ultimate baking guide* by Tim Jones

4. *what's in the oven?* by Laura Hall

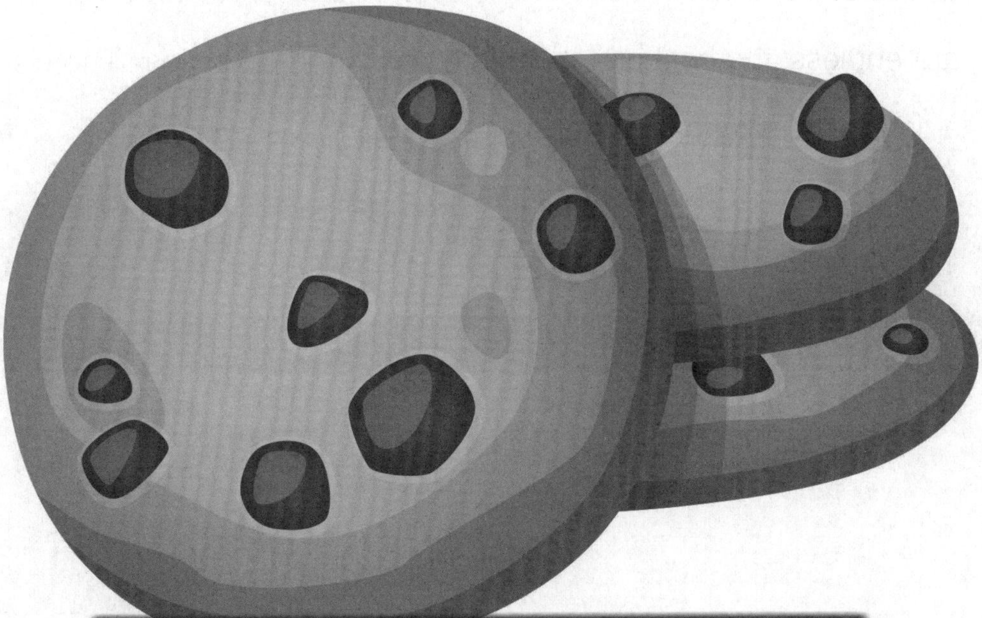

Boost Your Learning!

When writing titles, always capitalize the first and last words of the titles, nouns, adjectives, adverbs, and verbs, and words over five letters.

NAME: ______________________ **DATE:** ______________

Publishing: Cookies

Directions: Reread the opinion paragraph about cookies. Add one supporting detail to complete the paragraph.

Cookies are the best dessert. There are so many different types to choose from. They go well with a glass of milk. Dunking them is so much fun! ____. They are versatile and come in many sizes. The different ingredients are endless; the best are chocolate chips and sprinkles. There's a flavor and size for everyone.

This week I learned:

- how to identify nouns
- how to use pronouns
- how to capitalize book titles

 © Shell Education

NAME: ______________________ **DATE:** ________________

Directions: Read the statement. Then, write at least three statements in each column.

Ice cream is the best dessert.

Agree	Disagree

Drafting
Ice Cream

NAME: ____________________ **DATE:** ____________

Directions: Do you think ice cream is the best dessert? Draft an opinion paragraph explaining your thoughts. Give at least three reasons to support your opinion. Use your notes from page 159 to help you draft your opinion paragraph.

Cursive Practice

Directions: Use cursive to write your favorite ice cream flavor.

© Shell Education

NAME: ____________________ **DATE:** ________________

Directions: Use the (delete) symbol to correct pronouns that are used incorrectly.

My sister loves ice cream. He would eat it every day if my parents allowed it. Their favorite flavor is vanilla. She goes with everything, so it claims. They loves adding toppings of all varieties, including cherries. Them are her favorite!

Remember!

Use pronouns in your writing to vary sentences. It makes your writing more exciting.

Subject pronouns include *I, we, you, he, she, it*

Object pronouns include *me, us, you, him, her, it*

Time to Improve!

Go back to the draft you wrote on page 160. Did you include any pronouns? If you did use them, did you use them correctly? If you did not, fix them!

NAME: ______________________ **DATE:** ______________

Directions: Use the ≡ symbol to correct the capitalization errors in the book titles.

1. *one scoop, two scoops* by Sam Hunt
2. *the toppings* by Michael Green
3. *chocolate is a must* by Jeremy Lands
4. *how to make ice cream* by Lindsay Cooper

Quick Practice

Directions: Write the correct spellings of the plural nouns.

1. dessert ______________________
2. cherry ______________________

Time to Improve!

Go back to the draft you wrote on page 160. Check to make sure that you have correctly capitalized necessary words.

 © Shell Education

NAME: ______________________________ **DATE:** ____________________

Directions: Do you think ice cream is the best dessert? Write an opinion paragraph explaining your thoughts. Give at least three reasons to support your opinion.

____

____

____

____

____

____

____

____

____

____

____

NAME: ____________________ **DATE:** ____________________

Directions: Place check marks in the volcanoes that contain titles for narrative paragraphs. Then, answer the question.

Facts About Active Volcanoes

The Day the Volcano Erupted

Why Volcanoes Erupt

My Sailing Trip on a Volcano's Lava

Our Volcano Adventure

1. Explain why you marked specific volcanoes.

____

____

____

© Shell Education

NAME: ______________________ **DATE:** ________________

Directions: Check the paragraph for proper subject-verb agreement. There are three incorrect verbs. Write the verbs correctly on the lines below.

Matthew wait in suspense, as his teacher is about to announce the next science unit. His face beam when she reveals it's about volcanoes. Matthew know some facts but is intrigued and wants to learn more. The teacher explains how they will read books, watch science videos, and perform experiments to better understand the complex unit on volcanoes. Matthew can't wait to get started.

1. ______________________
2. ______________________
3. ______________________

Cursive Practice *abc*

Directions: Write the words *volcano* and *erupt* in cursive.

NAME: ____________________ **DATE:** ____________________

Revising
Active Volcanoes

Directions: Underline the subjects and circle the verbs in the sentences. Check for the correct subject-verb agreement. If the sentence is correct, write *Correct*. If a sentence needs correcting, rewrite it on the lines below. The first one is done for you.

1. The *volcano* causes damage when it erupts.

   Correct

2. Earth's plates shifts back and forth.

3. Lava flows out of a volcano.

4. Volcanic eruptions may sends ash high into the air.

5. Lava cool slowly.

 © Shell Education

NAME: ______________________ **DATE:** ________________

Directions: Use the ~~℘~~ symbol to correct the misspelled words in the sentences.

1. Sarah is excited to learn more abowt volcanoes.
2. Billy beleives the bigest problem is the destruction volcanoes may cause.
3. The class wants to no how many active volcanoes exist.
4. Mrs. Potter explanes the difference betwean active and dormant volcanoes.
5. The students are surprised to learn their are over 1,500 active volcanoes inn the world.

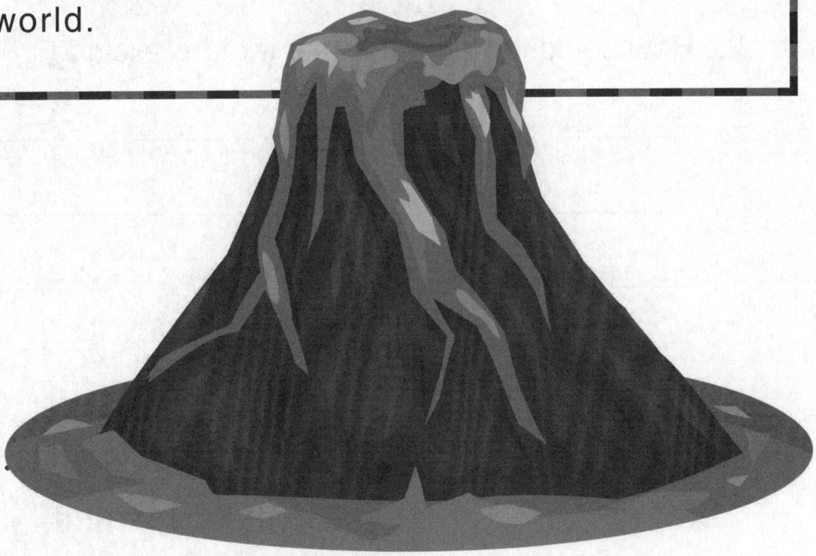

Quick Practice

Directions: Underline the adjectives in the sentences.

1. Red lava flows from active volcanoes.
2. Earth's crust is made up of huge slabs called plates.

NAME: ______________________ **DATE:** ________________

Directions: Read the paragraph. Then, answer the questions.

Matthew waits in suspense, as his teacher is about to announce the next science unit. His face beams when she reveals it's about volcanoes. Matthew knows some facts but is intrigued and wants to learn more. The teacher explains how they will read books, watch science videos, and perform experiments to better understand the complex unit on volcanoes. Matthew can't wait to get started.

1. What makes this a strong narrative paragraph?

____

____

____

2. How could the author make it more exciting?

____

____

____

This week I learned:

- how to use proper subject-verb agreements
- how to edit for spelling errors

 © Shell Education

NAME: ______________________ **DATE:** ________________

Directions: Read the sentence about dormant volcanoes. Then, use the chart below to plan out a narrative paragraph about visiting a dormant volcano.

Dormant volcanoes haven't erupted for a long time but could still erupt.

My Dormant Volcano Story
Title:
Characters ________________ ________________ ________________ ________________
Problem ________________ ________________ ________________ ________________ ________________
Solution ________________ ________________ ________________ ________________ ________________

NAME: ______________________ **DATE:** ______________

Directions: Imagine you are near a dormant volcano. Draft a narrative paragraph about your experience. Use your notes from page 169 to help you draft your paragraph.

Remember!

A strong narrative paragraph:

- includes an introductory and a concluding sentence
- uses sensory details to describe the experience
- makes it sound like a story

Cursive Practice

Directions: Use cursive to write two adjectives that describe a volcano.

© Shell Education

NAME: ____________________ **DATE:** ____________________

Directions: Write five complete sentences. Each sentence should use one subject and one verb from the chart. Think about subject-verb agreement when making your choices.

Subjects	Verbs
dormant volcanoes	form
scientists	shift
lava	flows
tectonic plates	erupt
volcanoes	think

1. ____________________
2. ____________________
3. ____________________
4. ____________________
5. ____________________

Time to Improve!

Go back to the draft you wrote on page 170. Check to make sure that all of your sentences have subject-verb agreement.

NAME: ____________________ **DATE:** ____________

Directions: Use the ℘ symbol to correct any misspelled words in the paragraph.

How amazing our volcanoes? Weather active, dormant, or extinct, they all have unique qualitys. They come in many shapes and sizes and vary in location. Sum are famous for their size and destruction, unfortunately. Others are famous for there beauty and function. Mauna Kea is won of the five volcanoes that make up the big island of Hawaii. Now that's one incredible volcano!

Time to Improve!

Go back to the draft you wrote on page 170. Check to make sure that all of your words are spelled correctly.

© Shell Education

NAME: ______________________ **DATE:** ________________

Directions: Imagine you are near a dormant volcano. Write a narrative paragraph about your experience. Remember to write in sequential order.

NAME: ______________________ **DATE:** ______________

Directions: Place check marks in the circles that have items you might need on a hike. Then, answer the question.

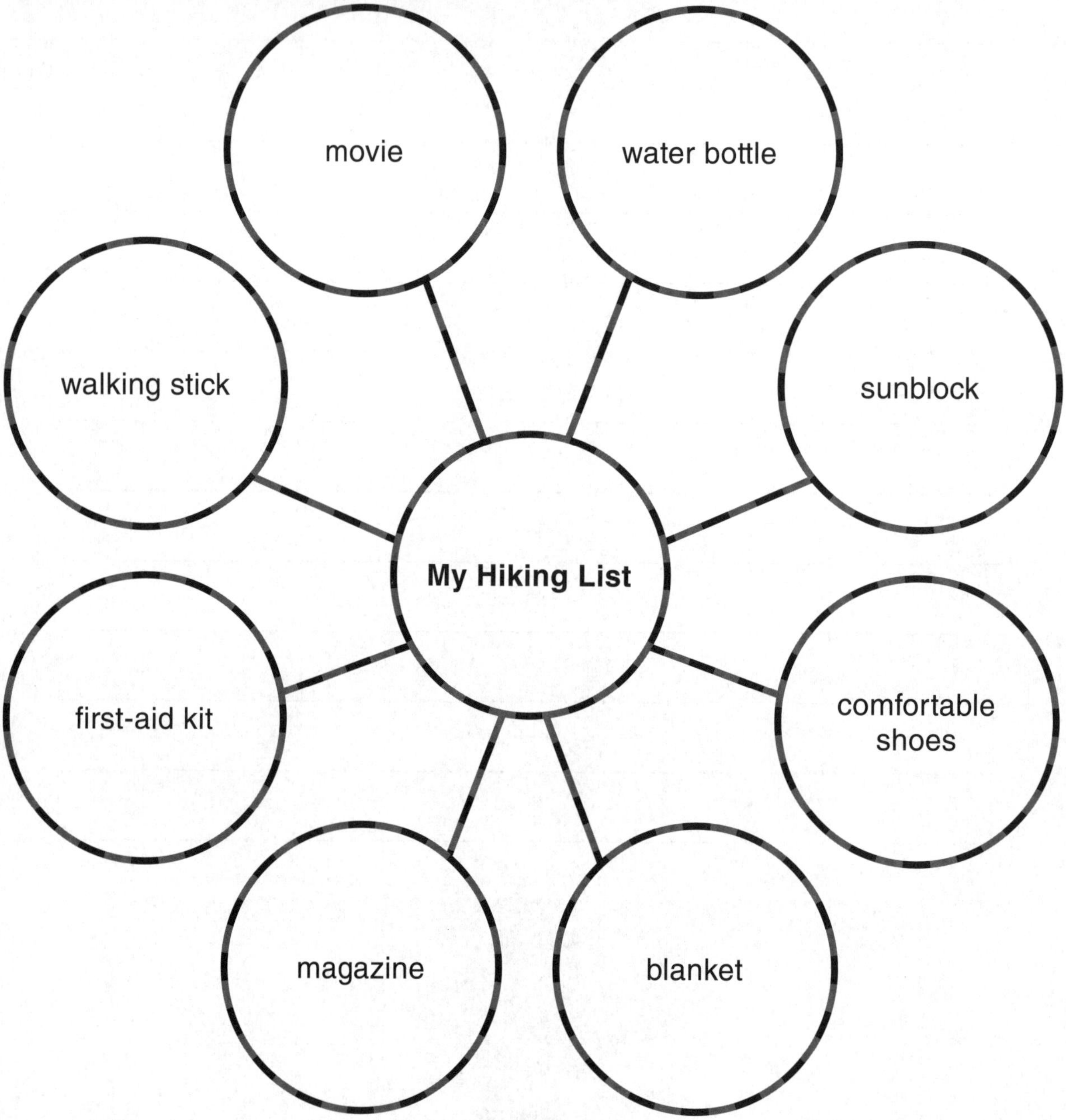

1. Do you think hiking is a fun activity? Why or why not?

____

____

____

 © Shell Education

NAME: ______________________ **DATE:** ________________

Directions: Read the paragraph. Circle the author's opinion. Then, underline the supporting details.

Hiking is a great outdoor activity. Some people enjoy it, but others prefer different outdoor activities such as running, bike riding, or swimming. Depending on the hiking trail, it can be flat or uphill. Either way, it takes a lot of energy. Hiking is very good exercise, and everyone should try it at least once.

Cursive Practice *abc*

Directions: Use cursive to write the words *hiking* and *nature*.

NAME: ______________________ **DATE:** ________________

Directions: Underline the past tense verbs in the sentences. Then, rewrite the verbs in present tense.

1. Liam loved hiking in the mountains.

   ____

2. Amy's dog, Jasper, had a hard time making it up the hills.

   ____

3. The trail was dark and shady.

   ____

4. A hiker rested under the shady oak tree.

   ____

5. Melissa and James were quite thirsty after their long hike.

   ____

Quick Practice

Directions: Fill in the blank with the correct comparative or superlative adjective.

1. The new trail was ______________ than the old trail. (long)
2. Sara had the ______________ water canteen in our group. (large)

 © Shell Education

NAME: ______________________ **DATE:** ________________

Directions: Use the ∨ symbol to add an apostrophe to each possessive noun.
Hint: There are both singular- and plural-possessive nouns.

1. The hikers shirt was full of sweat.
2. Sams water bottle started leaking halfway through the hike.
3. The boys dads enjoyed the shade after a long, hot hike.
4. Before Billy started hiking, he remembered the suns rays were extra strong. So he put sunscreen on his face.
5. Both of our dogs tongues were hanging out as they panted all the way home.

NAME: ______________________ **DATE:** ______________

Directions: Reread the paragraph about hiking. Delete and revise the sentences that do not fully support the topic. Rewrite a new and improved paragraph below.

Hiking is a great outdoor activity. Some people enjoy it, but others prefer different outdoor activities such as running, bike riding, or swimming. Depending on the hiking trail, it can be flat or uphill. Either way, it takes a lot of energy. Hiking is very good exercise, and everyone should try it at least once.

This week I learned:

- how to identify verbs
- how to change verb tenses when writing
- how to use possessive nouns

© Shell Education

NAME: ______________________________ **DATE:** ____________________

Directions: Some people like camping and some people don't. Fill out the chart with notes that support both views. Then, answer the question.

Why Camping Is Fun	Why Camping Is Not Fun

1. Do you think camping is fun?

____

NAME: ____________________ **DATE:** ____________

Drafting : Camping

Directions: Do you like camping? Draft an opinion paragraph explaining why you do or do not like camping. Include at least three reasons to support your opinion. Use your notes from page 179 to help you draft your opinion paragraph.

Remember!

A strong opinion paragraph includes:

- an introductory sentence
- details that support your opinion
- a concluding sentence

Cursive Practice

Directions: Complete the sentence. Then, use cursive to rewrite the sentence.

I prefer going ____________________.
(hiking/camping)

NAME: ______________________ **DATE:** ________________

Directions: Read the paragraph. Complete the sentences with past-tense verbs.

Camping was a fun experience. We ____________ the car and set up our tent as soon as we got there. We ____________ horseshoes and volleyball. My dad ____________ a campfire while my mom got dinner ready. We ____________ hamburgers and hot dogs. My favorite part was dessert because we roasted marshmallows and ____________ s'mores. Before bed, we told stories around the campfire. It was the best vacation ever!

Time to Improve!

Go back to the draft you wrote on page 180. Check to make sure that all of your verbs are the same tense. If they are not, correct them!

NAME: ____________________ **DATE:** ____________________

Directions: Rewrite the phrases using possessive nouns.

1. the flames of the fire

   ____

2. the clang of the horseshoe

   ____

3. the rays of the sun

   ____

4. the poles of the tent

   ____

Quick Practice

Directions: Use context clues to explain the meaning of the underlined word.

Mom and dad <u>pitched</u> the tent before dark because we needed a place to sleep.

____

Time to Improve!

Go back to the draft you wrote on page 180. Did you include any possessive nouns in your writing? If not, try to add some. If you did include them, make sure they are used correctly.

 © Shell Education

NAME: ______________________ **DATE:** ________________

Directions: Do you like camping? Write an opinion paragraph explaining why you do or do not like camping. Include at least three reasons to support your opinion.

NAME: ______________________ **DATE:** ______________

Directions: Place check marks in the books that contain items you would find in a public library.

librarians

radios

books

magazines

people

rides

library cards

computers

© Shell Education

NAME: ____________________ **DATE:** ____________

Directions: Read the paragraph. Circle the coordinating conjunctions within the paragraph. Then, answer the question.

A third-grade class arrives at the public library. Jade and Jake are excited to be at the library, but they can't find their library cards. Neither the teacher nor the librarian can find the cards, either. Meanwhile, the class does research on the computers or looks for additional books to check out. All are now lined up and ready to check out their material, when suddenly, Jade shouts, "Jake, our cards were in my back pocket the whole time!" The class barely leaves the public library, yet they can't wait to go back again soon.

1. How does adding conjunctions to compound sentences help the reader better understand the writing?

____

____

____

____

____

____

Remember!

Coordinating conjunctions connect words, phrases, and clauses.

Cursive Practice *abc*

Directions: Write the title of your favorite book in cursive.

____

____

NAME: ______________________ **DATE:** ______________

Revising
Public Library

Directions: Use the words in the Word Bank to replace the underlined words in the sentences. Use context clues in the sentences to help you.

Word Bank			
create	locate	excited	gathered

1. Jenny was thrilled to get two library books instead of one.

   ____

2. The librarian helped me find the book I was looking for.

   ____

3. Randy and his friends met at the library to study together.

   ____

4. The librarian had to make a new library card for Henry.

   ____

Quick Practice

Directions: Write the parts of speech that the bolded words are.

The **librarian** was helpful and friendly. ______________________

Johnny whispered **softly** as he spoke to his mother. ______________________

The clerk **gave** me a new library card. ______________________

 © Shell Education

NAME: ______________________ **DATE:** ________________

Directions: Use the ∧ symbol to add commas and the ∨ symbol to add quotation marks to the dialogue. Then, answer the question.

Mom, my library book is due said Molly. When can we go to the library?

We should have time tomorrow after school Mom replied.

I said I will get two books this time. I finished this one too quickly.

That sounds like a great idea. Just don't forget your library card this time Mom suggested.

I'm putting it in my backpack right now Molly said happily.

1. How does dialogue add to a narrative paragraph?

____

____

NAME: ______________________ **DATE:** ________________

Publishing
Public Library

Directions: Reread the paragraph. Then, answer the questions.

A third-grade class arrives at the public library. Jade and Jake are excited to be at the library, but they can't find their library cards. Neither the teacher nor the librarian can find the cards, either. Meanwhile, the class does research on the computers or looks for additional books to check out. Their time goes quickly, and all are now lined up ready to check out their material, when suddenly, Jade shouts, "Jake, our cards were in my back pocket the whole time!" The class barely leaves the public library, and yet they can't wait to go back again soon.

1. What makes this a strong narrative?

____

____

____

2. What improvements would you make to the narrative?

____

____

____

This week I learned:

- how to identify coordinating conjunctions
- how to use context clues to find meaning
- how to edit for commas and quotation marks

 © Shell Education

NAME: ____________________ **DATE:** ________________

Directions: Place check marks in the mailboxes that have people or things you might see inside of a post office.

trees

letters

packages

ice cream cones

postage stamps

envelopes

employees

dogs

NAME: ______________________ **DATE:** ______________

Directions: Imagine that you need to mail a package and have just arrived at the post office. What do you do next? How do you make sure your package gets mailed? Draft a narrative about your experience. Use your notes from page 189 to help you draft your narrative paragraph.

Remember!

A strong personal narrative:

- is about you
- has a beginning, a middle, and an end
- sounds like a story

Cursive Practice

Directions: Write the words *letter* and *package* in cursive.

© Shell Education

NAME: ______________________________ DATE: ____________________

Directions: Use context clues to find another word with a similar meaning to the bolded word in each sentence. Then, write the new words on the lines.

1. Mail carriers are responsible for delivering mail to **residences** six days a week.

   ____

2. The post office **relies** on the sale of postage, products, and services to fund its operations.

   ____

3. The mail clerk weighed the **parcel** to make sure enough postage was placed on it.

   ____

4. The post office gets quite **congested** during the holiday rush reason.

   ____

Time to Improve!

Go back to the draft you wrote on page 190. Look for words that can be replaced to make your writing more exciting.

NAME: ______________________ **DATE:** ________________

Editing

Post Office

Directions: Use the ⌇ symbol to eliminate any sentence that does not belong in the paragraph below.

My sister and I walked to the post office to mail our thank-you notes. It's only one block from our house, so my mom lets us walk together. There's a restaurant on the corner. I just had my ninth birthday party and was so thankful for all of my amazing gifts that I needed to send thank-you notes to all who came. To our surprise, there was a long line when we got to the post office. There was a big tree out front. We got in line, and luckily, a kind employee came up and talked to us. We told him why we were there, and he was so pleased with our thoughtfulness of sending thank-you notes that he took us right to the front of the line. My mom really likes writing notes. We paid for our postage, handed the thank-you notes to the gentleman, and were on our way back home before we knew it.

Time to Improve!

Go back to the draft you wrote on page 190. Check to make sure that all of your sentences relate to the topic. If they don't, cross them out or revise them.

© Shell Education

NAME: ______________________ **DATE:** ______________

Directions: Imagine that you need to mail a package and have just arrived at the post office. What do you do next? How do you make sure your package gets mailed? Write a narrative about your experience.

ANSWER KEY

The activity pages that do not have specific answers to them are not included in this answer key. Students' answers will vary on these activity pages, so check that students are staying on task.

Week 1: Desert Animals

Day 1 (page 14)

Students should check the following: Desert animals have adaptations that help them survive in the desert; Lizards hide under rocks to protect themselves from the sun; Most desert animals spend their time underground.

Day 2 (page 15)

1. Desert animals must adapt to extreme heat and lack of water.
2. The author is missing a concluding sentence.

Day 3 (page 16)

1. C
2. I—The camels **travel** over the sand dune.
3. I—The lizard **buries** himself under a rock.
4. I—A desert animal **adapts** to its surroundings.

Day 4 (page 17)

1. desert
2. live
3. Sandstorms
4. ways
5. some

Day 5 (page 18)

Verb corrections: is—are; drinks—drink; holds—hold

1. Example answer: The paragraph gives facts and details about the desert. It does not go off topic.

Week 2: Tundra Animals

Day 1 (page 19)

Students should check the following:
They have adaptations for survival.
They have minimal skin exposure to stay warm.
These animals either hibernate or migrate for the winter.
There is always a fluctuation in population.
There are about 48 different animals in the tundra.
The largest tundra animal is the polar bear.

Day 4 (page 22)

1. very
2. tails
3. rays
4. for

Day 5 (page 23)

See Informative/Explanatory Writing Rubric on page 203.

Week 3: Summer/Fall

Day 1 (page 24)

1. F
2. F
3. S
4. F
5. S
6. S
7. F
8. S

Day 2 (page 25)

Students should circle: Summer is the best time of the year.

Students should underline: Going to the beach, taking swimming lessons, and going on vacation are some of my favorites.

Day 3 (page 26)

1. Sara **learned** how to rake the leaves.
2. He **carved** the pumpkin on Saturday.
3. The children **went** to the beach with their parents.
4. Ben **played** with his beach ball at the pool.

Day 4 (page 27)

Sentences include: Going to the beach**,** taking swimming lessons**,** and going on vacation are some of my favorites; He loves going to the dog park**,** playing fetch**,** and swimming in the pool.

Day 5 (page 28)

1. The author gives her opinion that fall is the perfect season to enjoy the great outdoors.
2. The author includes reasons for why she thinks fall is the perfect season, such as hiking trails and playing soccer.

Week 4: Winter/Spring

Day 3 (page 31)

1. plants
2. fall
3. wear
4. hatch
5. drive

Day 4 (page 32)

1. I like to ski**,** snowboard**,** and build snowmen in the winter.
2. There's snow**,** rocks**,** and ice everywhere!
3. Flowers**,** trees**,** and bushes begin to bloom in the springtime.
4. You can see butterflies**,** birds**,** and bees flying around the garden.

Day 5 (page 33)

See Opinion Writing Rubric on page 202.

ANSWER KEY *(cont.)*

Week 5: Wild Animals

Day 2 (page 35)

Opinions: Wolves are excellent hunters; Their ability to work together is astounding.

Day 3 (page 36)

1. bigger
2. tallest
3. stronger
4. fastest
5. fiercer

Day 4 (page 37)

Capitalize: Some, Dolphins, There, Ocean, Pacific Ocean, Atlantic Ocean, Their

Day 5 (page 38)

1. Example answer: The author uses sentences such as, "Their ability to work together is astounding" and "Wolves who hunt in the Arctic have to travel longer distances than those in the forest."

Week 6: Pets

Day 1 (page 39)

Possible answers: has an owner, fed by humans, walked on a leash, lives in a cage.

Day 3 (page 41)

Possible adjectives: fuzzy, soft, large, furry, small

Day 4 (page 42)

Capitalize: Hamsters, They, Hamsters, They, Just

Day 5 (page 43)

See Opinion Writing Rubric on page 202.

Week 7: Continents

Day 1 (page 44)

Antarctica opinion: I really enjoy playing in the snow.

Africa opinion: The variety of wild animals you see on a safari is very cool.

North America opinion: The 50 states are all very interesting.

Asia opinion: I really like the traditions that Asian countries celebrate.

Day 2 (page 45)

Adjectives: second, largest, longest, largest, hot, quite. **Note:** You may wish to include articles as adjectives.

1. The adjective help make the writing more interesting.

Day 4 (page 47)

Spelling corrections: past, joined, Some, others, countries, moving, which

Day 5 (page 48)

1. The paragraph is filled with factual information about the topic, Africa.
2. A stronger paragraph may include information on the animals that live in Africa.

Week 8: Bodies of Water

Day 2 (page 50)

Possible answers: The Pacific Ocean is very large. Lake Superior is one of the Great Lakes in Michigan. The Nile River is the longest river in the world. The Atlantic Ocean touches the east coast of the United States.

Day 3 (page 51)

Incomplete sentences: Atlantic Ocean about half the size of Pacific Ocean; Many islands found within the Atlantic including the Bahamas and Greenland

Day 4 (page 52)

1. also
2. only
3. body
4. Sea
5. largest

Day 5 (page 53)

See Informative/Explanatory Writing Rubric on page 203.

Week 9: Birthdays

Day 2 (page 55)

anxious**ly**; careful**ly**; **re**do; usual**ly**; **mis**behaves; event**ful**

1. They help add details to the paragraph.

Day 3 (page 56)

1. peacefully
2. swiftly
3. happily
4. extremely
5. carefully

Day 4 (page 57)

1. **"**Listen up! It's time to cut the cake**,"** said Jacob's mom.
2. **"**This bounce house is so much fun**!"** cried Sam.
3. Jacob's mom said**, "**Don't forget your goodie bags**!"**
4. **"**This chocolate cake is delicious**,"** I said.

Day 5 (page 58)

Sara was so excited for her birthday party. Her grandparents were the first to arrive. Then came several friends and a few more family members. First, they played games, and musical chairs was the favorite. Sara enjoyed opening her gifts next. Lastly, everyone munched on some delicious chocolate cake.

ANSWER KEY *(cont.)*

Week 10: Holidays

Day 4 (page 62)

My favorite thing about the holidays is celebrating with my family. When it's time to eat my mom calls down, **"**Olivia, it's time for the feast.**"**

I respond with, **"**Hooray, I'm coming right now!**"**

I love baking special recipes with my grandma and singing traditional songs with my family that comes to visit from all over the country. We enjoy homemade dessert each night as we sit around and share memories from the past year. My grandmother repeatedly says, **"**It's just so great to see you. I've missed you!**"**

My family members call out, **"**We've missed you, too, Grandmother. Now let's make the best of it!**"**

She's not the only one who feels this way. I find myself thinking the same thing as I soak in the time with my loved ones.

Day 5 (page 63)

See Narrative Writing Rubric on page 204.

Week 11: Tornadoes

Day 1 (page 64)

dark, gloomy, large, funnel-shaped, disastrous

Day 2 (page 65)

twisters; rapidly; miles; rotate; tornadoes

Day 3 (page 66)

1. Correct as is.
2. The <u>air</u> **whirls** upward.
3. Correct as is
4. A <u>tornado</u> **touches** the ground.

Day 4 (page 67)

Capitalized: Sometimes; A; Kansas; Oklahoma; Texas; Tornadoes

Quick Practice:

1. huge, gray, empty
2. fifty, central

Week 12: Earthquakes

Day 1 (page 69)

1. F
2. O
3. F
4. F
5. F
6. F
7. O
8. F

Day 3 (page 71)

In order: Earth's crust, These plates, Some earthquakes

Day 4 (page 72)

1. The tectonic plates **shifted** back and forth, causing a small earthquake.
2. An earthquake is sometimes quite **terrifying**, and people panic.
3. **Mudslides** are common after a large earthquake because the soil has shifted.
4. Great damage can come from the **tremendous** force of an earthquake.
5. **Tsunami** waves can be quite large and can ruin entire cities or a small country.
6. The amount of damage an **earthquake** causes is based on its depth.

Day 5 (page 73)

See Informative/Explanatory Writing Rubric on page 203.

Week 13: Air Travel

Day 1 (page 74)

Student answers will vary. Possible answers: helicopter—small, hovers, no wings; airplane—large, has wings, carries many passengers; both—fly, can transfer people

Day 2 (page 75)

Student answers will vary. Possible sentences: Vince couldn't believe how quickly the time had passed; Vince was proud of himself for keeping busy and staying brave; The landing was smooth, and Vince was happy to be back on the ground.

Day 3 (page 76)

1. Landon thinks helicopters are fascinating because they can hover motionless in the air.
2. Since helicopters are very useful means of transportation, Officer Frank is able to protect people with them.

Week 14: Land Travel

Day 1 (page 79)

Student answers will vary. Possible answers: car, truck, bike, skateboard, van, bus, train, subway.

Day 3 (page 81)

Student answers will vary. Possible answers: ride, stop, pedal, push, turn

Day 4 (page 82)

Student answers will vary. Possible answers:

1. quickly
2. sternly
3. slowly
4. carefully
5. immediately

Day 5 (page 83)

See Narrative Writing Rubric on page 204.

ANSWER KEY *(cont.)*

Week 15: Superheroes

Day 1 (page 84)

Possible answers: brave, tough, helpful, heroic, kind

Day 2 (page 85)

Are a great part of entertainment history; Enjoy reading about superheroes.

Day 3 (page 86)

1. A superhero's strength is great.
2. A superhero's power is the best part about him or her.
3. Superheroes' battles are always intense.

Quick Practice:

1. A noun is a person, place, or thing.
2. A verb shows action or a state of being.

Day 4 (page 87)

1. is
2. are, make
3. is, gives
4. is
5. is

Day 5 (page 88)

1. It states a person's thoughts or feelings.
2. Context clues may include: great part of entertainment history; enjoy reading about superheroes; making them quite interesting; thrilling experience

Week 16: Villains

Day 1 (page 89)

Possible answers include: strong, determined, intelligent, flexible, brave

Day 3 (page 91)

1. A **villain's powers** are evil.
2. It's wonderful that the **villains' enemies** defeat them.
3. It's interesting how the **villains' egos** can cause them to lose a battle.
4. A **villain's evil** can be harmful to those around him or her.

Day 4 (page 92)

made—make; was—is; thought—think; got—get

Day 5 (page 93)

See Opinion Writing Rubric on page 202.

Week 17: Grand Canyon

Day 1 (page 94)

1. fact
2. opinion
3. fact
4. fact
5. opinion

Day 2 (page 95)

The Grand Canyon located in Arizona; Have lived around the Grand Canyon for thousands of years.

Day 3 (page 96)

1. cleanest
2. narrowest
3. deeper
4. most
5. widest

Quick Practice: People/take helicopter rides into the canyon.

Day 4 (page 97)

northurn—northern; won—one; maid—made; threw—through

Quick Practice:

1. pyramids
2. countries
3. bodies

Day 5 (page 98)

The Grand Canyon is locates (**located**) in Arizona. It's 277 miles (446 kilometers) long. It is one of the large (**largest**) canyons in the world. The Colorado River runs threw (**through**) the Grand Canyon. Native Americans have lived around the Grand Canyon for thousands of years. People enjoys (**enjoy**) visiting this beautiful place. Visitors often hike the canyon or go rafting on the river.

Week 18: Egyptian Pyramids

Day 1 (page 99)

Complete sentences: They vary in size. It took a long time to build each pyramid. The pyramids are fascinating. The base of a pyramid is square.

Day 3 (page 101)

1. most
2. largest
3. tallest
4. longer
5. smaller

Day 4 (page 102)

There are many unique facts about the pyramids. The Great Pyramid of **Giza** points to the north. The pyramids of **Egypt** were all built to the west of the **Nile** River. The base of the pyramid was always a perfect square. The pyramids were built mostly of limestone. **There** were traps and curses put on the pyramids to try to keep the robbers out. **It's** unbelievable how advanced the culture was thousands of years ago.

Day 5 (page 103)

See Informative/Explanatory Writing Rubric on page 203.

ANSWER KEY *(cont.)*

Week 19: Thomas Edison

Day 3 (page 106)

1. Thomas Edison may be the greatest inventor in history, having over 1,000 patents.
2. Thomas Edison built a research laboratory for the purpose of inventing.
3. Thomas Edison was born in Milan, Ohio, but later moved to Michigan.

Day 4 (page 107)

Menlo Park**,** NJ; Milan**,** OH; Port Huron**,** MI; Rocky Point**,** CA

Week 20: Benjamin Franklin

Day 3 (page 111)

1. simple
2. compound
3. compound
4. simple
5. simple

Day 4 (page 112)

1. Boston**,** Massachusetts
2. London**,** England
3. Albany**,** New York
4. Philadelphia**,** Pennsylvania

Day 5 (page 113)

See Narrative Writing Rubric on page 204.

Week 21: Octopuses

Day 1 (page 114)

Octopuses have eight arms; An octopus' tentacles allow it to grab objects; Octopuses come in all sorts of colors; An octopus has no bones in its body.

Day 3 (page 116)

1. and
2. but
3. nor
4. so
5. but

Day 4 (page 117)

Spelling errors: sum—some, weighs—ways, hyde—hide, cents—sense, sea—see

Day 5 (page 118)

Possible answers include: The areas around the eyes, arms, and suckers may get dark so the octopus appears more threatening; Octopus can reach speeds of 25 miles per hour, but cannot maintain this speed for too long.

Week 22: Sharks

Day 1 (page 119)

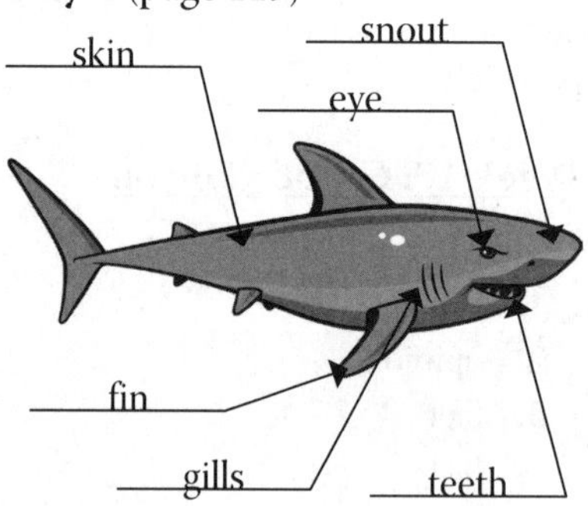

Day 3 (page 121)

1. and
2. so
3. yet

Day 4 (page 122)

1. makeing—making
2. childs—children
3. powerfull—powerful
4. tipe—type
5. tooths—teeth

Day 5 (page 123)

See Informative/Explanatory Writing Rubric on page 203.

Week 23: Planets

Day 1 (page 124)

Students should star the following: There are eight planets in our solar system. Earth is one of the planets in our solar system. Jupiter is the largest planet. Mars is nicknamed the Red Planet because of its red-color dirt. Mercury is the closest planet to the sun. The outer planets consist of Jupiter, Saturn, Uranus, and Neptune.

Day 2 (page 125)

Students should cross out the following: I like rockets; People enjoy watching space movies; Would you travel to space?

Day 3 (page 126)

1. fewer
2. brightest
3. more
4. largest
5. biggest
6. lightest

Quick Practice:

1. Mercury**,** Venus**,** Earth**,**
2. comets**,** dust**,** moons**,**

Day 4 (page 127)

Corrections in order as they appear: Planets—planets; pluto—Pluto; sometimes—Sometimes; venus—Venus; jupiter—Jupiter; uranus—Uranus; Rock—rock; jupiter—Jupiter

Day 5 (page 128)

There are eight planets in our solar system, including our planet, Earth. Jupiter is the largest planet. Mars is nicknamed the Red Planet because of its red-color dirt. Mercury and Venus are the closest planets to the sun. Venus's yellow clouds reflect the sun's light brightly. The outer planets consist of Jupiter, Saturn, Uranus, and Neptune. An interesting fact about Saturn is its many moons; it has about 53 known moons.

 © Shell Education

ANSWER KEY *(cont.)*

Week 24: Sun and Moon

Day 1 (page 129)

Possible answers: The sun is a star. The sun is very hot. The moon is bright at night. We can see the moon at night.

Day 3 (page 131)

1. largest
2. tallest
3. stronger
4. closer
5. bigger

Quick Practice:

1. sun's
2. Earth's
3. moon's

Day 4 (page 132)

1. **The** first **person** to set foot on the **moon** was **Neil Armstrong**.
2. A lunar eclipse occurs when **Earth** is between the **sun** and the **moon**.
3. **The moon** orbits **Earth** every 27.3 days.
4. **Many** civilizations have worshipped the **sun** because of its great importance.
5. **A** solar eclipse **occurs** when the **moon** is between Earth and the sun.

Day 5 (page 133)

See Informative/Explanatory Writing Rubric on page 203.

Week 25: Eric Carle

Day 1 (page 134)

Students should check mark the following: Which book that you have written is the most meaningful to you?; What other jobs have you had?; What is the title of the first book you wrote?; When did you start drawing?

Day 2 (page 135)

1. The dialogue brings interest and helps the reader understand what is happening between the characters.

Day 3 (page 136)

Used—uses, created—creates, painted—paints, created—creates, made—make

Quick Practice: watch, bat, trunk

Day 4 (page 137)

"I want to be an author when I grow up," said Molly.
"You can be anything you want, as long as you work hard," Eric Carle stated.
"I am willing to work extra hard. I promise," Molly said with a smile.
"One day, you'll be reading a book by the famous Molly," she announced.

Week 26: J.K. Rowling

Day 3 (page 141)

is—was, enjoyes—enjoyed, goes—went, is—was, goes—went

Day 4 (page 142)

1. "I want to meet J.K. Rowling!" exclaimed Samantha.
2. Brian whispered, "I wish I were a famous author."
3. "Writing takes a lot of concentration," said Mrs. Temple.
4. "I still need to edit and revise my story," Mary said. "I cannot publish it quite yet."
5. "It's hard to believe J.K. Rowling went from being unemployed to being a millionaire in just five years," Mom stated.

Quick Practice: exhausted, overwhelmed

Day 5 (page 143)

See Narrative Writing Rubric on page 204.

Week 27: Butterflies

Day 1 (page 144)

egg, larvae, pupa, adult

Day 2 (page 145)

Opinions: Butterflies are peaceful to watch; The four stages of metamorphosis are interesting and complex.

Day 3 (page 146)

Possible answers: beautiful, interesting, colorful, small

Day 4 (page 147)

1. brightly
2. slowly
3. patiently
4. carefully

Day 5 (page 148)

1. No, it needs to have at least three strong details to support the opinion that butterflies are so amazing.
2. Get rid of the simple facts (such as six legs and three body parts) and add more unique and less-known facts to the paragraph.

Week 28: Bees

Day 3 (page 151)

Possible aswers include:

1. It's hard to believe a queen bee can lay up to 1,500 eggs a day.
2. It seems unfair to have only one queen bee in an entire colony.

Day 5 (page 153)

See Opinion Writing Rubric on page 202.

ANSWER KEY *(cont.)*

Week 29: Cookies

Day 2 (page 155)

Singular nouns: dessert, glass, milk, flavor, size

Plural nouns: cookies, types, sizes, ingredients, chocolate chips, sprinkles

Day 3 (page 156)

1. them
2. Her
3. them

Quick Practice:

1. True
2. False—Commas are used to separate the date from the year

Day 4 (page 157)

1. Cookies Are Yummy
2. Baking Bliss
3. The Ultimate Baking Guide
4. What's in the Oven?

Day 5 (page 158)

Possible answers: A tall glass of milk is a must; Some are large, and some are miniature size.

Week 30: Ice Cream

Day 3 (page 161)

My sister loves ice cream. **She** would eat it everyday if my parents allowed it. **Her** favorite flavor is vanilla. **It** goes with everything, so **she** claims. **She** loves adding toppings of all varieties, including cherries. **They** are her favorite!

Day 4 (page 162)

1. One Scoop, Two Scoops
2. The Toppings
3. Chocolate is a Must
4. How to Make Ice Cream

Quick Practice:

1. desserts
2. cherries

Day 5 (page 163)

See Opinion Writing Rubric on page 202.

Week 31: Active Volcanoes

Day 1 (page 164)

Students should mark the following titles: The Day the Volcano Erupted, Our Volcano Adventure, My Sailing Trip on a Volcano's Lava.

Day 2 (page 165)

1. wait—waits
2. beam—beams
3. know—knows

Day 3 (page 166)

1. Correct
2. Earth's plates **shift** back and forth.
3. Correct
4. Volcanic eruptions **may send** ash high into the air.
5. Lava **cools** slowly.

Day 4 (page 167)

1. about
2. believes, biggest
3. know
4. explains, between
5. there, in

Quick Practice:

1. Red, active
2. huge

Week 32: Dormant Volcanoes

Day 3 (page 171)

Possible subject-verb pairs: dormant volcanoes (do not) erupt; scientists think; lava flows; tectonic plates shift; volcanoes form

Day 4 (page 172)

Corrections in order as they appear: our—are; Weather—Whether; qualitys—qualities; Sum—Some; there—their; won—one

Day 5 (page 173)

See Narrative Writing Rubric on page 204.

Week 33: Hiking

Day 1 (page 174)

Students should mark the following circles: walking stick, water bottle, sunblock, first-aid kit, comfortable shoes.

Day 2 (page 175)

Students should circle: Hiking is a great outdoor activity.

Students' underlining will vary.

Day 3 (page 176)

1. loves
2. has
3. is
4. rests
5. are

Quick Practice:

1. longer
2. largest

Day 4 (page 177)

1. hiker's
2. Sam's
3. boys'
4. sun's
5. dogs'

Day 5 (page 178)

Students should delete the following sentences: Some people enjoy it, but others prefer different outdoor activities such as running, bike riding, or swimming.

ANSWER KEY *(cont.)*

Week 34: Camping

Day 3 (page 181)

Possible answers include: unpacked, played, started, grilled, made, was

Day 4 (page 182)

Student answers will vary slightly.
Possessive nouns:

1. the fire's flames
2. the horseshoe's clang
3. the sun's rays
4. the tent's poles

Quick Practice: *pitched* means to set up or put up.

Day 5 (page 183)

See Opinion Writing Rubric on page 202.

Week 35: Public Library

Day 1 (page 184)

Students should check the following: librarians, books, magazines, people, library cards, computers

Day 2 (page 185)

Students should circle *but*, *or*, and *yet*.

1. Adding conjunctions to compound sentences helps the reader understand because conjunctions help connect related ideas or phrases.

Day 3 (page 186)

1. excited
2. locate
3. gathered
4. create

Quick Practice: noun, adverb, verb

Day 4 (page 187)

"Mom, my library book is due," said Molly. "When can we go to the library?"

"We should have time tomorrow after school," Mom replied.

I said "I will get two books this time. I finished this one too quickly."

"That sounds like a great idea. Just don't forget your library card this time," Mom suggested.

"I'm putting it in my backpack right now," Molly said happily.

1. Dialogue adds interest to the writing.

Day 5 (page 188)

Possible answers include:

1. The narrative has characters, setting, a problem, and a solution.
2. Maybe add some detail about why they are there, more specifically what type of project they're working on.

Week 36: Post Office

Day 1 (page 189)

Mailboxes that should be checked include: letters, packages, postage stamps, envelopes, employees

Day 3 (page 191)

Possible answers include:

1. homes/houses
2. depends/counts
3. package/box
4. crowded/full/packed

Day 4 (page 192)

Sentences that don't belong: There's a restaurant on the corner.; There was a big tree out front.; My mom really likes writing notes.

Day 5 (page 193)

See Narrative Writing Rubric on page 204.

OPINION WRITING RUBRIC

Directions: Evaluate students' work in each category by circling one number in each row. Students have opportunities to score up to five points in each row and up to 15 points total.

	Exceptional Writing	Quality Writing	Developing Writing
Focus and Organization	Clearly states an opinion that is relevant to the topic. Demonstrates clear understanding of the intended audience and purpose of the piece. Organizes ideas in a purposeful way and includes an introduction, a detailed body, and a conclusion.	States an opinion that is relevant to the topic. Demonstrates some understanding of the intended audience and purpose of the piece. Organizes ideas and includes an introduction, a body, and a conclusion.	States an unclear opinion that is not fully relevant to the topic. Demonstrates little understanding of the intended audience or purpose of the piece. Does not include an introduction, a body, or a conclusion.
Points	5 4	3 2	1 2
Written Expression	Uses descriptive and precise language with clarity and intention. Maintains a consistent voice and uses an appropriate tone that supports meaning. Uses multiple sentence types and transitions smoothly between ideas.	Uses a broad vocabulary. Maintains a consistent voice and supports a tone and feeling through language. Varies sentence length and word choices.	Uses a limited or an unvaried vocabulary. Provides an inconsistent or a weak voice and tone. Provides little to no variation in sentence type and length.
Points	5 4	3 2	1 2
Language Conventions	Capitalizes, punctuates, and spells accurately. Demonstrates complete thoughts within sentences, with accurate subject-verb agreement. Uses paragraphs appropriately and with clear purpose.	Capitalizes, punctuates, and spells accurately. Demonstrates complete thoughts within sentences and appropriate grammar. Paragraphs are properly divided and supported.	Incorrectly capitalizes, punctuates, and spells. Uses fragmented or run-on sentences. Utilizes poor grammar overall. Paragraphs are poorly divided and developed.
Points	5 4	3 2	1 2

Total Points: ____________________

 © Shell Education

INFORMATIVE/EXPLANATORY WRITING RUBRIC

Directions: Evaluate students' work in each category by circling one number in each row. Students have opportunities to score up to five points in each row and up to 15 points total.

	Exceptional Writing	Quality Writing	Developing Writing
Focus and Organization	Clearly states the topic and purposefully develops it throughout the writing. Demonstrates clear understanding of the intended audience and purpose of the piece. Organizes the information into a well-supported introduction, body, and conclusion.	States the topic and develops it throughout the writing. Demonstrates some understanding of the intended audience and purpose of the piece. Organizes the information into an introduction, body, and conclusion.	Does not state the topic and/ or develop it throughout the writing. Demonstrates little understanding of the intended audience or purpose of the piece. Fails to organize the information into an introduction, body, or conclusion.
Points	5 4	3 2	1 2
Written Expression	Uses descriptive and precise language with clarity and intention. Maintains a consistent voice and uses an appropriate tone that supports meaning. Uses multiple sentence types and transitions smoothly between ideas.	Uses a broad vocabulary. Maintains a consistent voice and supports a tone and feeling through language. Varies sentence length and word choices.	Uses a limited or an unvaried vocabulary. Provides an inconsistent or a weak voice and tone. Provides little to no variation in sentence type and length.
Points	5 4	3 2	1 2
Language Conventions	Capitalizes, punctuates, and spells accurately. Demonstrates complete thoughts within sentences, with accurate subject-verb agreement. Uses paragraphs appropriately and with clear purpose.	Capitalizes, punctuates, and spells accurately. Demonstrates complete thoughts within sentences and appropriate grammar. Paragraphs are properly divided and supported.	Incorrectly capitalizes, punctuates, and spells. Uses fragmented or run-on sentences. Utilizes poor grammar overall. Paragraphs are poorly divided and developed.
Points	5 4	3 2	1 2

Total Points: ____________________

NARRATIVE WRITING RUBRIC

Directions: Evaluate students' work in each category by circling one number in each row. Students have opportunities to score up to five points in each row and up to 15 points total.

	Exceptional Writing	Quality Writing	Developing Writing
Focus and Organization	Identifies the topic of the story and maintains the focus throughout the writing. Develops clear settings, a strong plot, and interesting characters. Demonstrates clear understanding of the intended audience and purpose of the piece. Engages the reader from the opening hook through the middle to the conclusion.	Identifies the topic of the story, but has some trouble maintaining the focus throughout the writing. Develops settings, a plot, and characters. Demonstrates some understanding of the intended audience and purpose of the piece. Includes an interesting opening, a strong story, and a conclusion.	Fails to identify the topic of the story or maintain focus throughout the writing. Does not develop strong settings, plot, or characters. Demonstrates little understanding of the intended audience or purpose of the piece. Provides lack of clarity in the beginning, middle, and/or conclusion.
Points	5 4	3 2	1 2
Written Expression	Uses descriptive and precise language with clarity and intention. Maintains a consistent voice and uses an appropriate tone that supports meaning. Uses multiple sentence types and transitions smoothly between ideas.	Uses a broad vocabulary. Maintains a consistent voice and supports a tone and feeling through language. Varies sentence length and word choices.	Uses a limited or an unvaried vocabulary. Provides an inconsistent or a weak voice and tone. Provides little to no variation in sentence type and length.
Points	5 4	3 2	1 2
Language Conventions	Capitalizes, punctuates, and spells accurately. Demonstrates complete thoughts within sentences, with accurate subject-verb agreement. Uses paragraphs appropriately and with clear purpose.	Capitalizes, punctuates, and spells accurately. Demonstrates complete thoughts within sentences and appropriate grammar. Paragraphs are properly divided and supported.	Incorrectly capitalizes, punctuates, and spells. Uses fragmented or run-on sentences. Utilizes poor grammar overall. Paragraphs are poorly divided and developed.
Points	5 4	3 2	1 2

Total Points: ____________________

 © Shell Education

OPINION WRITING ANALYSIS

Directions: Record each student's rubric scores (page 202) in the appropriate columns. Add the totals every two weeks and record the sums in the Total Scores column. You can view: (1) which students are not understanding the opinion genre and (2) how students progress after multiple encounters with the opinion genre.

	Week 4	Week 6	Week 16	Week 28	Week 30	Week 34	Total Scores
Student Name							
Average Classroom Score							

INFORMATIVE/EXPLANATORY WRITING ANALYSIS

Directions: Record each student's rubric score (page 203) in the appropriate columns. Add the totals every two weeks and record the sums in the Total Scores column. You can view: (1) which students are not understanding the informative/explanatory genre and (2) how students progress after multiple encounters with the informative/explanatory genre.

	Week 2	Week 8	Week 12	Week 18	Week 22	Week 24	Total Scores
Student Name							
Average Classroom Score							

NARRATIVE WRITING ANALYSIS

Directions: Record each student's rubric score (page 204) in the appropriate columns. Add the totals every two weeks and record the sums in the Total Scores column. You can view: (1) which students are not understanding the narrative genre and (2) how students progress after multiple encounters with the narrative genre.

	Week 10	Week 14	Week 20	Week 26	Week 32	Week 36	Total Scores
Student Name							
Average Classroom Score							

THE WRITING PROCESS

STEP 1: PREWRITING

Think about the topic. Brainstorm ideas, and plan what you want to include in your writing.

STEP 2: DRAFTING

Use your brainstormed ideas to write a first draft. Don't worry about errors. This will be a rough draft.

STEP 3: REVISING

Read your rough draft. Think about the vocabulary you used and how your writing is organized. Then, make the appropriate changes to improve your written piece.

STEP 4: EDITING

Reread your revised draft. Check for errors in spelling, punctuation, and grammar. Use editing marks to correct the errors.

STEP 5: PUBLISHING

Create a final version of your piece, including the corrections from the edited version. Be sure to reread your work for any errors.

© Shell Education

EDITING MARKS

Editing Marks	Symbol Names	Example
≡	capitalization symbol	david gobbled up the grapes.
/	lowercase symbol	My mother hugged Me when I Came Home.
⊙	insert period symbol	The clouds danced in the sky⊙
sp ◯	check spelling symbol	I laffed at the story.
∽	transpose symbol	How you are?
^	insert symbol	Would you ^please pass the pizza?
^,	insert comma symbol	I have two cats, two dogs^, and a goldfish.
“ ” ∨ ∨	insert quotations symbol	“That's amazing,” she shouted.
deletion mark	deletion symbol	Will you call call me on the phone tonight?
¶	new paragraph symbol	… in the tree. ¶After lunch, I spent the day…
#	add space symbol	I ran tothe tree.

OPINION WRITING TIPS

Ask yourself . . .	Remember . . .
Do I have a strong belief in my opinion so that I can convince others to believe the same?	Make sure you can back up your opinion with specific examples.
Have I stated my opinion in a way that grabs the reader's attention?	Begin with a question or a bold statement that includes your opinion.
Do I have at least three reasons based on facts for my opinion?	Include at least three solid reasons why the reader should agree with you.
Do I have an example for each reason that strengthens my argument?	Each reason must be followed by one strong example.
Do I have a logical order to my writing?	Don't bounce around. Focus on a logical order to present each reason and example.
Am I using smooth transitions to connect my thoughts and help my writing flow?	Use transition words like *first*, *in addition to*, *another reason*, and *most important*.
Does my conclusion restate my opinion?	Do not forget to restate your opinion in the final sentence.
Have I used correct spelling, grammar, and punctuation?	Revisit what you have written. Then, check for mistakes.

INFORMATIVE/EXPLANATORY WRITING TIPS

Ask yourself . . .	Remember . . .
Do I provide enough information on the topic?	Make sure to include facts about the topic in your writing so that the reader is informed.
Have I narrowed the focus of the topic?	Choose one aspect of the topic that you want to write about.
Does my writing have a hook?	Begin with a strong topic sentence that grabs the reader's attention.
Is my information presented in a logical order?	Do not bounce around. Present each topic sentence at the beginning of a paragraph and add details.
Have I included enough information that the reader will be interested in learning even more?	End with a strong sentence that makes the reader want to learn more about the subject.
Have I used correct spelling, grammar, and punctuation?	Revisit what you have written. Then, check for mistakes.

NARRATIVE WRITING TIPS

Ask yourself . . .	Remember . . .
Am I the main character? Is the story told from my point of view?	You are in the story, telling where you are, what you see, who you are with, and what you do.
Does my story have a hook?	Include an exciting introductory sentence that makes the reader want to continue reading.
Does my story make sense and have a beginning, a middle, and an end?	Do not bounce around. Focus on a logical order of how the experience happened.
Am I using transitions to connect my thoughts and help the writing flow?	Use transition words like *first*, *next*, *then*, *another*, and *finally*.
Am I including rich details and sensory language to help paint a picture in the reader's mind?	Use lots of adjectives, and incorporate figurative language, such as metaphors and similes, to make your story come to life.
Does my conclusion summarize the main idea?	Incorporate a sentence or two that reflects on what you have written.
Have I used correct spelling, grammar, and punctuation?	Revisit what you have written. Then, check for mistakes.

© Shell Education

Opinion Writing

Informative/Explanatory Writing

Narrative Writing

DIGITAL RESOURCES

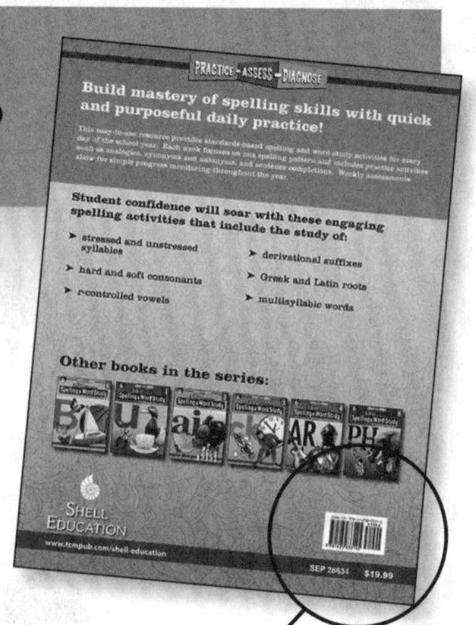

Accessing the Digital Resources

The digital resources can be downloaded by following these steps:

1. Go to **www.tcmpub.com/digital**
2. Sign in or create an account.
3. Click **Redeem Content** and enter the ISBN number, located on page 2 and the back cover, into the appropriate field on the website.
4. Respond to the prompts using the book to view your account and available digital content.
5. Choose the digital resources you would like to download. You can download all the files at once, or you can download a specific group of files.

ISBN:
9781425815264

Please note: Some files provided for download have large file sizes. Download times for these larger files will vary based on your download speed.

CONTENTS OF THE DIGITAL RESOURCES

Teacher Resources

- Informative/Explanatory Writing Analysis
- Narrative Writing Analysis
- Opinion Writing Analysis
- Writing Rubric
- Writing Signs

Student Resources

- Peer/Self-Editing Checklist
- Editing Marks
- Practice Pages
- The Writing Process
- Writing Prompts
- Writing Tips

© Shell Education